T0147150

MEN,
WAKE UP!

WHAT YOU DON'T KNOW COULD BE KILLING YOUR RELATIONSHIPS

ANTHONY D. MCKINLEY

WESTBOW
PRESS®
A DIVISION OF THOMAS NELSON
& ZONDERVAN

Copyright © 2023 Anthony D. McKinley.

All rights reserved. No part of this book may be used or reproduced by any means, graphic, electronic, or mechanical, including photocopying, recording, taping or by any information storage retrieval system without the written permission of the author except in the case of brief quotations embodied in critical articles and reviews.

This book is a work of non-fiction. Unless otherwise noted, the author and the publisher make no explicit guarantees as to the accuracy of the information contained in this book and in some cases, names of people and places have been altered to protect their privacy.

WestBow Press books may be ordered through booksellers or by contacting:

WestBow Press
A Division of Thomas Nelson & Zondervan
1663 Liberty Drive
Bloomington, IN 47403
www.westbowpress.com
844-714-3454

Because of the dynamic nature of the Internet, any web addresses or links contained in this book may have changed since publication and may no longer be valid. The views expressed in this work are solely those of the author and do not necessarily reflect the views of the publisher, and the publisher hereby disclaims any responsibility for them.

Any people depicted in stock imagery provided by Getty Images are models, and such images are being used for illustrative purposes only.
Certain stock imagery © Getty Images.

Scripture taken from the King James Version of the Bible.

ISBN: 978-1-6642-8162-2 (sc)
ISBN: 978-1-6642-8161-5 (hc)
ISBN: 978-1-6642-8160-8 (e)

Library of Congress Control Number: 2022919303

Print information available on the last page.

WestBow Press rev. date: 02/22/2023

The greatest gift of life is being able to love yourself and your family, and to raise your children.

Being a father is one of the most important roles that any man can ever fill, and the payoff is worth the time you invest.

Contents

Special Thanks and Acknowledgements

Thanks to God, the Creator of my life for creating the life of my Mother whose love and determination taught me never to give up; my children who are the fuel of my determination to live and who hold a special place in my heart and soul; my family and friends who encourage me along this journey; and to my passed beloved Grandfather Lawrence McKinley, Jr. who help me save my life and whose spirit of order, understanding, wisdom and charity now is within me to pass on to my children and others.

On this journey I endured a traumatic brain injury, ruptured knee injury (I only can bend 70 in range) and a loss of vision with double vision sight. The doctors said I would not recover, and I informed them that I know a God that set high and looks low and will restore me. Although, I still suffer from stress, discouragement, depression and internal pain; and I also have challenges with relationships, but I work on being positive and thoughtful.

I want to acknowledge two people that have really been there for me since the injury: my sister Kristal Grove who always keep it real and keeps me grounded, and one of my best friend Charles Traylor. When I was challenge with relationship and wanting to give up on self, he would remind me of who I am and would say, "if anyone can, you can, and I believe in you". We all need people to redirect us and encourage us in times of storms and these two never gave up and reminded me I can do it.

Thanks for believing in me.

I thank God that I can type with my eyes closed and read from my thoughts or I would have never completed this book.

CHAPTER ONE

WHAT IS A MAN?

What is a man? The act of a male in man's role.

Men struggle with their identities when there is no father to teach them about manhood or demonstrate manhood. The father has to love his family and children enough to teach them, guide them, and give them the mental knowledge and physical resources they need. This is so they can work toward having a life to live and having dominion over themselves, their property, and their finances.

Genesis 1:26–27 (KJV) states, "God said, 'Let us make man in our image, after our likeness, and let them have dominion over the fish of the sea, and over the fowl of the air, and over the cattle, and over all the earth and over every creeping thing that creepeth upon the earth.'" It is important to know your history, purpose, and role in life. Women, children, and society need you to do well as a man, son, brother, husband, and father. When a male and a female create unity and the two come together and create a child, it is then called a family. And when a child is born, it does not matter whether you are married or not.

The infrastructure then needs to be established because the child is now manifested. Regardless of relationship status (married or not), the titles shift from "male" and "female" to "mother" and "father." After the child is manifested, the responsibility is upon both man and woman, who are now called "parents."

The parents are the caretakers of the child, as it pertains to providing the basic needs for the child, until they can provide for themselves as adults. Both parents' goals are to love, teach, guide, protect, discipline, reinforce living principles, and produce a law-abiding citizen. It is believed that if the parents are married, this is a goal made by both of them for their children. Unfortunately, in America we live in a society that is moving from togetherness to separatism within the family structure, and America is rapidly influencing the world in this regard.

According to Single Mother Statistic and 2021 U.S. Census Bureau, out of about 11 million single parent families with children under the age of 18, nearly 80 percent were headed by single mothers. This means that the father is not present daily in the house to honor the parental goal.

On April 27, 2018, Pew Research Center published an article titled "Fact Tank: News in the Numbers" by Gretchen Livingston. It reported that "one-third of US children are living with an unmarried parent. This has doubled since 1968, from 13 percent to 32 percent in 2017. And 3 percent are not living with either parent." All told, twenty-four million US children younger than eighteen are living with an unmarried parent, and most (fifteen million) are living with a single mother. This is in comparison to the five million children who live with cohabiting parents and the three million that live with single fathers.

Based on the above data, this means that *men* are not present in the homes of single mothers, which also means that single mothers and their children are now vulnerable prey. The safety of these mothers and children is now in question because there is no protector in the house to secure the family. The message, men, is *wake up!*

I will elaborate. For example, men, let's say you have a daughter and you and the mother are not together in the home or in a relationship. You pick up your daughter every other weekend for the first six years of her life. Then you get a new job, and the lady that you are serious with loves to travel. So you take her on trips for romantic encounters. But your relationship with your daughter moves from biweekly visits to visits once a month or whenever you can manage them because of new demands in your life. This type of change occurs for about five years, and everything appears to be fine. There are no complaints from the child's mother.

Eventually, picking up your daughter moves to holidays and when you have time. But your daughter begins to find other things to do, and she finds herself in love with an older high school boy. Your daughter begins having morning sickness, only to find out that she is pregnant. She tells you, and you are infuriated. Then she says, "Daddy, why are you so mad? Just be happy for me." Fathers, remember when all of us were young boys and girls. We were ready and in a hurry to become adults so that we could move out on our own, to live and be free from our parents' home!

The one thing we did not know was that home was actually a safe haven from the world of predators, liars, rapists, and pedophiles who lurk and prey on the innocent, naive, vulnerable, and lonely. So remember this when you have children. They will have the same curiosity about moving out.

Men, I beg of you, please wake up! Just because your children don't live in your house and under your roof does not mean that your presence and responsibilities are not needed. Your children came from your bloodline, and you are blessed to have been given the opportunity to be a father to your children.

Your children are a blessing from God or from yourself, whichever you believe. By having children, you and the mother are given this assignment, as both of you are the parents, to raise, train, and educate your children, protect them from others, and ensure that they can become productive citizens. This is a great *responsibility*, and you will be charged with it *forever*.

Therefore, your parental role should be served with pride, dignity, and love. This is the opportunity of a lifetime, and nothing in the world is greater.

So, fathers, wake up and be fathers to your children and men to your families. This is what you were born to do, and this is one of the innate abilities and desires within your DNA. It is designed for you to push toward being honored and respected by your family, and especially your children. When you do the right things and become an old man, your family will take care of you.

As a man and father, it is my belief that these character traits need to be explored and elaborated on. I know that we are logical and that the more information we have, the better we can examine it and make better decisions as to why we need to change.

There are five roles that are key to being a father. I have identified and defined them so that we can add to our knowledge and better understand ourselves. Peace be unto you.

Five Roles of a Father

1. God-Fearing / Spiritual Leader: This is a man of morals, truth, and honesty. He is truthful to his commitments and attentive to himself and his family's needs.
2. Provider: This man has dominion and can subdue, replenish, be fruitful, and multiply all aspects of the family's needs, including mental, physical, spiritual, and financial needs.
3. Teacher: This man is able to demonstrate, teach, love, and show self-control and recognition.
4. Protector: This is a man of courage and displays strength, compassion, and tenderness. He has a mindset of a warrior that builds and protects in the best interest of his family while preparing for the future.
5. Disciplinarian: This is a man that directs, trains, and prepares the family. He is one who is gentle and firm and loves unconditionally, through the ups and downs.

God-Fearing / Spiritual Leader

A God-fearing leader or spiritual leader is a man of morals, truth, and honesty regarding his commitments. And he is attentive to himself and his family's needs. He has a core belief that helps him to remain focused, and he possesses a set of principles that ensure his behavior is safe.

It is said that having morals and ethics is what keeps a man centered and focused. But others believe that there is a God or greater/superior universal being. They believe in a creator that is greater than humans and animals, who created all things that exist. Yet there are religious and spiritual reading materials and practices that are considered good if they encourage positive behavior, peace, and humor within self, family, and other human beings.

But why is this important? Having mental and physical stability, as well as self-control, is essential for *all* humans—and specifically for *men*, because of man's untamed and immoral behavior. And when a man is not focused on his family or protecting them at all costs, idle things come into play.

Having faith is one thing, but having it for the right reasons sustains the mind. And it's very important that men learn to forgive. Forgiving is very important to *men* of morals and understanding. To lead a family requires being focused on family values and having a plan for life. This will help reduce high-risk behavior.

Provider

The provider has dominion and can subdue, replenish, be fruitful, and multiply all aspects of the family's needs. This includes mental, physical, spiritual, and financial needs. As providers, men should have an ultimate goal. To say you are a provider is another way of saying you are self-sufficient and capable of taking care of your lifestyle.

Let me be specific. A man should be preparing to be a man and a father in a family and to take care of his family as a provider. A man's goal should not be about being single and living his best life as if he doesn't have a family. That is why it is important that a man plans and prepares for his future, for the things to come. Planning means writing down your ideal lifestyle that you want for yourself and for your family.

Preparing for your life means putting in tasks in place and setting completion dates for implementation.

A provider should do the following to achieve life's successes on all four levels (L1-L5):

L1: Attend and high school, complete college or trade school or open a business, and save for retirement.

L2: Attend and graduate from a graduate school master's degree program, trade or certification program, or career advancement position, or open a second business if it is profitable, and save for retirement.

L3: Open another business if it is profitable and move toward a franchise. Earn a PhD degree, advance to a managerial or executive position (such as a vice president, or chief executive officer), and save for retirement.

L4: Seek ownership and training to do what you are doing and franchise it or get a pension for retirement and live off of your savings.

L5: Start a new career and invest your money into your end-of-life career and teach your family members.

Life is filled with many education and ownership opportunities to advance your lifestyle and growth. It is important to understand that your life as a man and a provider is very important to the existence of humanity. And if you are not contributing to yourself, your family, and your community, then your life is a lie and you are living in vain; you are also selfish and lack understanding about life and how we evolve to greater heights as human beings. Why? Being a provider means being able to give to self, family, children, and others who are in need of assistance.

Your family is to be covered; that is the first rule of life, because that is providing and protecting what is yours. Life begins after understanding and establishing this understanding within yourself as a man.

What does a provider provide for his family (wife, children, and other relatives)? A provider provides stability in the areas of being a voice of reason, love and kindness in situations that may arise (good and bad), financial contributions that support the family's needs, safety, a home, food for nourishment, and sexual intimacy to his wife. He also prepares the family for future investments and endeavors to create wealth.

Being able to prepare a lifestyle for the family is very important to the future of the family. Men, this is not a task for you to have to do by yourself; this is a task that is or should be cultivated within the family's structure. If it is not already cultivated, you can create the opportunity, but you have to remain focused on your intent and the goal. Your intent in doing this is not for self alone but rather for the betterment of the family.

If you are a man that has lost trust from the family, you have to repeatedly do things to reestablish trust until you have changed. Your family, too, have to change their minds about you and your actions. In this case, trust is earned until it is actually proven for the right reasons as you love and build your family.

Men, I want to remind you of an innate ability that is within you and has been deterred by other learned conditions that have you believing a lie. The lie is that you don't matter and that you are not needed. Here is the truth: You were born to build and provide together with your family members. You can alter the culture of your family through family events that unify and build a kingdom for the family to dwell and grow in. Also, for the prosperity of today's lifestyle, you can establish a future promised for your children to walk in and to be in control of as business owners.

Men, wake up! This is your calling and a chance to be leaders while you reap the benefits because of love and your intentions. Remember: you are not built to do it by yourselves; if there is a family task, then everyone has to work toward the common goal for the same reasons—family and love.

All the degrees, money, and status do not amount to the love and time you can give your children while you relieve their mother. Her ability to trust you means that she can move on with hope to loving again, because her family is secure.

As a man, to be a provider, you must also provide emotional support and build trust within the family. Men have to respect and love all their children and treat them the same with their love and time. Men, we have to respect children's mothers so that we can be in the loop of things that we are not aware usually of.

Part of being a provider is also maintaining strong communication with respect for everyone—especially the mothers in families. They know everything that men sometimes take for granted. You still are the provider, and you still protect your children when things are good and when things are bad. That is your role and responsibility, so own it and be it forever. That is what a real provider does. It is done for the children and family involved. Whether you are with the children's mother or not, she is still family, and it is your role as a provider to respect her at all times and do it out of the spirit of love. Men, wake up!

Men, wake up and realize your true destiny and your power to lead your families!

Teacher

A teacher is a man who is able to demonstrate and teach love, self-control, and recognition. Being a teacher requires the ability to lead by example, to act with patience, to listen with kindness, to speak with care, and to love doing it. As a teacher, you must have these capabilities to demonstrate to your children what a teacher and father looks like. Why? You are the first teacher that your children will know before going to school, which means you are the first impression in the eyes of your child's life. How you position yourself as a father in your child's life is very important, because if we don't teach our children, then they won't be taught with love, and then any other person will be able to influence our children without our permission or knowledge.

This is a scary and serious thought that should bug and bother men with regard to their pride. Men, be careful trusting your child around others in public or in relationships that their mothers move on to be in, because you are not with her or the family. For example, suppose you and your child are in line to take pictures and you left your bag on a chair. Now you notice that you are in a long line and don't want to wait any longer, so you ask the person behind you to watch your child while you go fewer than ten steps to get your bag. This is the wrong thing to do on all levels. You should never trust a stranger with your child. Why? Because your child is listening and watching. If you do this, your child will grow up being super friendly with and trusting of strangers, not knowing better. So watch what you do and say around your children and around strangers, because they don't understand the risks involved in being too trustworthy with strangers. Remember this: when your child says, "people are nice," this is a problem, because that is being naive regarding the difference between someone who is being genuinely nice and someone who is a predator that preys on children by pretending to be nice. Being too friendly can cost you your child's life!

The following is based on a real story:

A middle school called a mother and told her to come to the school ASAP because her daughter wouldn't stop crying and they didn't know what was wrong with her. So she rushed to the school and asked to speak to the principal. The principal came and said, "Let's talk in my office before seeing your daughter in order to give you an update of what we know. Right now your daughter is in the nurse's office, waiting." The mother then said, "So what happened?" The principal said, "All I know is that the teacher said that your daughter wanted to go to the bathroom right after coming into to the room, and when your daughter came back to the room, she was crying profusely. Then the teacher contacted me, and I spoke to your daughter. At that time she was not responding, and so I called you." The mother said, "Okay, I want to see my daughter now, please." The mother hugged her daughter and asked her what happened, and she said that she wanted to go home. The mother told the principal that she was taking her daughter home because she was acting scared. So the mother got home and comforted her daughter; however, she did not call and tell the father.

Years later, the daughter was in high school when three girls tried to take advantage of her in the bathroom, and she ran to the principal's office to report it. They had her talk to the school nurse and then called her mother and left a message. Afterward, the daughter called her dad and told him to come and pick her up from school because three girls had tried to take advantage of her innocence as a girl but she had gotten away. The father arrived at school, and they left. The father said, "I want you to take a physical and get examined if that is fine," and she agreed. The father called the mother and left a message about the event and stated where they were headed. Shortly after, the mother arrived while the daughter was in the examining room.

As the doctor was examining the daughter, he asked her if she had ever had sex before, and she said no. But after he conducted the examination, he had some news for her parents. The doctor went to speak to the parents about what he had discovered, which concerned him. The doctor then said that their daughter was either a regular masturbator and was very aggressive or she was not being 100 percent truthful.

The doctor said, "With your approval, I would like to have some psychological tests done," and the parents agreed. The mother went by herself to talk with her daughter. The daughter was not wanting to talk and did not see what the big deal was, and she asked, "Can we go home now?" The mother asked, "Have you had sexual intercourse?" The daughter said, "No, and besides, what I do with my body is my business. Leave me alone. Let's go." As they were leaving, she told her father, "Not right now; we can talk tomorrow." He said, "Okay, okay."

The next day, the father went to visit his daughter, and he asked her whether there was anything he could get for her. She said, "I know you want to know what is going on; if you go and get something to eat and drink while I smoke, I will tell you when you come back."

When he returned, she told him the following:

"In middle school, after you dropped me off at school and left, I waited by the principal's office to ask if I could use the older kids' bathroom, because I had to go very bad. Out of the blue, the principal approached me and asked if I was okay. I told him I needed to use the bathroom really badly, and he said, 'Come on with me.' After I used the bathroom, he picked me up and said, 'Listen to me; you are so pretty like your mother, and that smile is so pretty too. Do you like your mother?' 'Yes,' I said, 'I love my mother.' He asked if I wanted to be like my mother. And I said yes. 'Do you want me to help you?' he asked, and I said, 'Yes. I want to be just like my mother.' He said, "Then we need to meet every Monday morning." After around two weeks more of meeting on Mondays, he asked me if I was ready to be a woman like my mother, and I said yes. He did things to me that I did not consent to.

"Then he asked me to meet him at his house, and I told Mother that I was going to the movies. I started having relations with him because he said it would make me feel like a woman and be like Mother. So I am a woman now, and that is that. I am a woman, I am like my mother, and I'm happy with him."

Moments later, the phone rang. The father picked up the phone. It was the doctor, and he asked for her to come to the office for the results.

Both parents were present at the meeting, and the doctor said that the daughter was two months pregnant. The parents cried, and the daughter yelled, "How did this happen? I'm not married." She turned to her parents and said, "I'm so sorry, and I should have said no. I just wanted to fit in with the others and be like Mother." The parents hugged her and said, "It was not your fault, and it will be all right."

Protector

A protector is a man of courage who displays strength, compassion, and tenderness and has the mindset of a warrior. A protector builds and protects with the best interests of the family in mind and prepares for the future. A protector is someone who is honest, ethical, trustworthy, faithful, and dependable. He honors his words and time, is able to do what's right, has the ability to communicate to his family all aspects of things, and, lastly, is willing to endure and protect his family at all costs.

Most men are under the impression that being a protector means beating someone for being disrespectful to him, his girl, his child, or his family. This is the truth about how men feel; they are overprotective of people that mean the most to their hearts or people that they love dearly. However, this type of protection is almost an innate quality that is within most males and becomes even more pronounced when a male becomes a father. So this is nothing to work on. But problems arise when a man is not around to protect his family. Men, we should protect our families at all costs until we die. This does not mean not holding others accountable for the wrong actions that a man or family member takes, but it does mean saying no to anyone who even thinks that he or she is going to harm one's family. Yet how we handle such situations is what matters most.

Men, we have to be smart about the dumb stuff that we do and make sure that we don't end up in jail or dead. Why? Because your death would leave your family in a vulnerable position to be attacked, as there would not be a protector around to protect them. So men, be smart about your dumb stuff, and please listen, for we have been a part of the problem for so long. So let's do better as men when it comes to our women and children.

Unfortunately, men who are not staying in the same households as their children and their mothers also believe that the mothers should do all the work. All the while, they get to be free to go and come as they please, as if it is a choice. This is wrong all the way. Men, wake up. You know that you're wrong, but you choose not to do the right things because of ignorance and foolishness. Men, we are born to lead our families, and especially our children.

When you are not protecting your children, you are disregarding them, which means you are neglecting your children's lives. There is a need for support and love from fathers, and when it is not there, the results can be devastating or catastrophic to children. Just think of how a child sees and thinks of himself or herself. This is a very important role for fathers. They are to prevent emotional and mental breakdown in their children.

Fathers, when you don't come around, your boys or girls will be lost and in search of love from anyone that can dictate it with authority, such as a parent—specifically an absent parent. By the time a child with an absent father is sixteen, he or she has already formulated an opinion of his or her father, without his or her mother's influence. However, it is the father's absence in these cases that causes the child to perceive his or her dad in a negative light.

If you ever hear your child or any child say, "My dad doesn't listen, and he doesn't care about me and my feelings," you will have to ask yourself why. Being a protector as a father, it is your role to ensure the safety of your family and that the care of your children is secured. If your child is saying this to you and you don't respond or think that it is serious, then you are in denial of your child's love for you and how much you are disappointing him or her. Don't let this fester. As your child grows and learns, deal with it out of love by listening to him or her and discussing it with your family.

It takes a village to raise children. Your children's perception of their father should be that their father is always there and that he is in their lives. Men, please get it into your minds that your children are learning and that they don't know anything except what you demonstrate to them, because they won't know anything until they come to the realization of things on their own as they get older. As a man and a protector, you are to protect, teach, and guide conversations to ensure that at least your child understands life from your point of view, because your responsibility is to act on behalf of the best interests of your children, their mother, and your family.

Men, you, as protectors, are examples of what a man is to your children, and sometimes to the mother, too, owing to the absence of a father in the lives of their children. Remember: what you don't discuss, exemplify, or teach to your child, may steer that child to learn information from someone else. And this could ultimately end up being his or her truth, which unfortunately can be misleading or manipulative and can have an unpleasant outcome as compared to the outcome of them learning the information you would have given them.

Information or instruction coming from you as a child's parent at least gives you comfort in knowing you are impacting your child and giving your best to hopefully prevent your child from having some bad experiences. Men, this a great thing. We are born to love, teach, and be protectors of the people and things that we love, and the most important should always be our ladies, our children, and our families. So utilize your power within your family and give advice to your children and other children in your family, especially when they need it during times of hardship or confusion about life.

The flip side to this is that if you don't protect and have conversations with your children, then who will? Are you willing to give that power to a stranger? Remember this statement: Anything is possible at the will of a predator! What this means to me is that when you leave the mother and the child, you leave room for any sick-minded person to enter your family's life because she or he comes across as passionate, loving, gentle, and kind. But that person may have a hidden agenda to seek and destroy for personal gain and control.

Men, wake up. Protect your families. You are *needed* by your families! Men, it is imperative that you be available every day. And understand that are no breaks when it comes to raising a child. Parenting is a twenty-four-hour responsibility. The parents must be there and available for both good and bad challenges. Your wisdom becomes the love that your children need to see and hear for comfort. Every child should be blessed to have two parents that raise them on a daily basis. Be the man you were born to be and that you desire to be. Men, wake up; you're needed!

Men, assume the power that comes with being fathers. It will not be easy, but it is rewarding to your character and to your maturity. The determination of whether you receive this power and respect it is based on your ability. But you must will it unto you believe it!

Gene A. Getz, the author of *The Measure of a Man*, wrote, "Our ability to be humble and kind is tested even further in our relationship with our children. A self-willed father can devastate and discourage his children. Though this is true for both parents, it is particularly applicable to fathers ... a self-centered, self-willed father can easily create intense anger and resentment in his children. This should not surprise us, because this kind of behavior creates anger and resentment in all of us."

Men, wake up! Your families need you every day that they have life. Men, we get a break while the women are doing their jobs and our jobs, too, as parents. Wake up and be a man that loves your family and makes it work by staying and enduring. You can do anything that you want to do when you put your heart in it for the right reasons with faith in yourself and your abilities.

If you are in a relationship in which there are no children and you are not happy, then end the relationship, especially if the two of you are not willing to work together. I say this because there are no responsibilities involved; you both deserve to be happy.

You need a real woman who cares about your well-being and who loves you. Just make sure that it is not you that is causing the problems because of previous hurt feelings and other relationships. All relationships requires endurance and the willingness to maintain them. If you can't do that, then you don't need to be in a relationship and you need to work on yourself and your personal development. The measure of a man is what others think of him. It does matter!

Disciplinarian

A disciplinarian is a man that teaches, directs, trains, and prepares the family. He is gentle, firm, and loves unconditionally. A disciplinarian is all of the above and is nonviolent, caring, nurturing, not argumentative, trustful, and loving, and doesn't cause separation.

According to *Webster's Dictionary*, a disciplinarian is one who enforces or believes in strict discipline. In the King James Bible, Proverbs 23:3 states, "Withhold not correction from the child; for if thou beat him with a rod, he shall not die." This biblical statement is so general that people interpreted it to justify abuse. So what I want to do is make sense of both of these statements when it comes to being a disciplinarian from a realistic point of view.

As a disciplinarian, it is important that you know that your role as a father is very sensitive and much needed. This role is loved and disliked by the mother and children, because correction by discipline is never a good feeling—especially when it comes to using a rod. I want to show you how this position is an honorable position, because you are automatically given the role and you should assume the role out of love and support.

The reason the mother and children don't like discipline is because of the strictness or the punishment in and of itself. That alone can be devastating to the imagination, especially if one has a past experience of abuse.

The truth of the matter is that being a disciplinarian requires a father to know that a situation is a teachable moment or nurturing moment. Being a supportive and gentle explainer or being the disciplinarian can be done in many ways, such as strict punishment, a weekly restriction, or spankings. All of these forms of discipline are needed when properly applied. You should never discipline out of anger, stress, or to be argumentative, and discipline should never be carried out violently.

Being a father means being loving to your children as a role model. Showing and explaining things to your children as a religious moral or God-fearing man, provider, protector, and teacher is what makes you a great disciplinarian and a loving father. Men, you are called to be a great father and a great role model. Show this to your children. Men, Wake Up!

Fathers, how you display your discipline to your children will determine how your children perceive you as a men and a father. Raising a child is more than a passive hobby; it is a full-time responsibility, and it is done by both parents. Fatherhood is one of the greatest success stories that you will ever tell, but you have to prove yourself in this role by being present daily.

CHAPTER TWO

THE ROLE OF A MAN

ccording to *Webster's Dictionary*, a man is "an adult male human. A human regardless of sex or age; a person. A human or an adult male human belonging to a specific occupation, nationality or other category."

> The steps of a good man are ordered by the Lord; and he delight in his way. (Psalm 32:23 KJV).

> A perfect man means an exemplary human being, who is superior and exalted, or any other inference of the sort. (Al-Islam.org: Part 1The Perfection)

It is believed that the role of a man is to be a God-fearing and loving provider, a teacher, a disciplinarian, and a protector. Being this type of man take years of practice. Some say, "How can you practice something that you have no knowledge of doing or any examples of why it is important to do?" This is a valid question and concern, and that is why I am writing this book—to give you knowledge and power so you can assume the position as a man for your family. The power to be a good man is achieved through being responsible, enduring, and fighting to protect what is yours.

A weakness is not having good intentions but rather doing things that are meant to do or cause harm to others. One of the hardest things that we as humans struggle with is admitting when we don't know something. Admitting that you don't know something is a strength, especially when you do something to change it.

Logically processing being a protector and fighting to do right and good for self, family, and the future bears an expensive cost that every person should reap a benefit from. If you don't do anything, then there is a cost of separation filled with mental and emotional disorders, as well as financial hardship. Having the power of knowing means being willing to sharpen the iron of knowledge with others striving to have lives filled with pleasure and love for family.

Being a Man

There are many people that populate the world, and everyone is racing to the top to be number one, the king of the hill. Even if you are on top or are the king and you won the race, the question is, Can you stay at the top? In other words, are you prepared to perpetuate and do the things necessary to stay on top as the king? Why is this state of mind important to a man? Winning does matter, and it is determined by your willingness to prove to yourself and others that you exist and that your life matters as a person and a man. Other people are like cheerleaders, and they will encourage you and push you to do better because they see your greatness and have a strong desire for you to achieve success as a man.

A winner has to walk into the light and prove to everyone, including himself, that he is on top. Why? So that others will see his greatness and they will desire to do the same in their areas of interest. A man has to have grit to endure all the things that comes his way. "Grit" is another word for mental toughness. To be an effective winner, you have the propensity to work, show your best self, and endure the ups and downs. Mental toughness requires the ability to maintain and seek for better ways to advance and improve your abilities. When you win, it makes everyone push to prepare for the next competition. A man has to be able to prove himself worthy to live and eat.

Men of Endurance

As a man, this was the area in my personal development where I was lacking, and I failed at it. Now that I am reflecting over my previous relationships—those involving friends, dating, family, and marriage—I know better. I am striving to do better, and it is very hard. Why? No one ever taught me; I had to learn it from inspirational insight and experiences.

A man must learn to endure life situations and learn from his mistakes and his failures. It is important to know that life is weighed on the shoulders of men. Why? Men should strive to seek for wisdom and guidance, and they should be the rocks that hold their families together during challenging times. Why? Because innately, men want to be the go-to guys, the people others call for advice, the people that others can rely on. Lastly, every man wants to be "the man!" Although men love this expression, it is unfortunately not the opinion of many women. It is also not a direct reflection on the men that stand their ground throughout the hard times.

Be present in good and bad times with family. Women may not understand the hardships that men endure, but one thing they do understand is not having a choice and being forced into being a single parent or enduring some other unforeseen situation. Men, wake up! If you are working all the time, then you're not spending time with your family or giving the mother a break. Parenting is a twenty-four-hour daily engagement. The strength of a man is present when you are present.

Fathers, remember this word: "self-preservation." According to *Webster's Dictionary*, self-preservation is "the protection of one-self from harm or distractions; the instinct for individual preservation; the innate desire to stay alive." It's imperative that you, as a protector securing the family's future, teach your family about self-preservation. In addition, fathers need to talk to their children about stranger danger, which means you teach them that no one should ever touch them in certain areas on their bodies. Reiterate this for the first seven to ten years of a child's life and explain why it is important. Fathers, wake up! Just because you're not living with the mother of your children does not mean that you should not raise your children and do your part. It takes two parents to raise a child, and both you and the mother have to be on the same page as it pertains to the well-being of the child's condition both mentally and physically.

Men, Wake Up; Teach Your Children!

An article in *Fatherly* magazine titled "How to teach Stranger Danger with Fact instead of Fear" by Matthew Utley, updated on August 13, 2019, states that "Stranger Danger" prepares kids for exaggerated threats, teaches consent, and helps them in any situation.

"The most important thing that parents need to know is that 93% of sexual abuse against children is perpetrated by those known to the child-meaning family, friends and those they know in their environment, like teachers and coaches," explains Elizabeth Jeglic, PhD, a professor of psychology at the City University of New York Graduate Center and author of *Protecting Your Child from Sexual Abuse.*

A man is one who teaches safety and awareness to his family. Remember, men: when you're not living in the house with your children, you are getting off the hook regarding being a responsible parent. Plus you get to enjoy your time and pleasure to do other things freely while the mother of your children is caring, teaching, and planting seeds of goodness into your children. Wake up! Being a man means remembering that it takes two parents to raise a child, and you as a man should always treat the mother of your children and the children accordingly. Be present and involved!

This is when "the man" can do better and show up. This is how you can cultivate your family by inviting the mother of your children to family events and special occasions. Family is all-inclusive. All parents should be able to do things together whether a father and mother are together or not. If the mother of your children has another man or husband, invite him as well. Being inclusive with all family members, especially the children's mother, is important to the safety, education, and well-being of children to ensure that all communication is expressed out of love through parenting. Men, remember to get your family closer.

Why? They depend on you because you are the protector of them. So assume this position out of love, peace, patience, and understanding with wisdom.

Note: Your love must be one of patience with others, because we are individuals; but keep your intent to love foremost, and in time, through patience, it will pay off. Men, wake up!

CHAPTER THREE

THE TRANSITION OF A MAN

A Call to Manhood

A call to manhood occurs when a man accepts his calling to move from boyhood into manhood, to be a watchman over his family, and to assist with securing the needs of the family. This is done through communicating, meeting financial needs, having family gatherings, and speaking with the other elders for direction. The call to manhood covers an array of transitions and mental changes.

A call to manhood occurs when a boy reaches a certain age and he has to take on more responsibilities to prove that he is not a child and that he has learned the necessity of how to live an independent life outside of his family home. I know this sounds old and outdated in this modern era, but it is true even to this day. It remains unspoken in certain ethnic groups, however, and because of the lack of unity, structure, and communication, this could be one of the reasons why men and women aren't even thinking about being married and why others are getting divorced.

The process of the call to manhood is called a rite of passage. The purpose of a rite of passage is tradition. Rites and ceremonies that are culturally specific can enable individuals to have opportunities to prosper and be productive citizens. As a man, it is critical that you develop your personality, character, and career choices, and learn the operational vernacular. Men should purchase land and become entrepreneurial owners to become self-sustaining. As a self-sustaining young adult man, you need to invest in yourself, own land, and build wealth as a provider. How does this impact your life? According to the text in the book titled *The Real Enemy: The Inner Me*, I state, "If you don't plan your own life then others will have a plan for you and it may not have anything to do with your will or destiny. So being selfish when it comes to your life is a positive mind state to have in order to help yourself."

Men, it is even more important to have a personal plan for your life to show value to yourselves, your families, and your future children. Being a man is more than work, having fun, having sex, and making babies that are not being properly raised, trained, or cared for. Being a man is being attached to a family that cares and loves each other through the good and bad times. Knowing this information is more valuable than having an attitude or feeling that someone disrespected you and doesn't love you the way you feel you need to be loved or respected. This information is for *you* as a *man* to come to the realization that you have a choice to change things in your family and impact them positively, even when there is hurt and dysfunction within the structure.

Being a man means doing hard things with a purpose and with determination for yourself to be in a family, being someone who takes the lead, and being a responsible person that knows his family's needs even though the family is not perfect.

When you do things from the heart and you know those things are not normal but are needed, then just do them in silence. Do them with a charitable mind and heart. You have the love within you to do them even knowing that you may not get a thank-you in return. Doing things without an expectation comes from unconditional love, but doing them with a consciousness of knowing that no apology is needed means understanding that doing them from the heart is more important.

Giving Up Is the Problem

My Child, My Responsibility

Men, one event (incident) can change the course of your life forever, so be wise in your decisions, because your family rely on your presence, your leadership, and your support.

At one time in life, you, the man, and your lady are dating, living life spontaneously, careless and having fun, with no real responsibilities. Then you find yourself in a sexual relationship with someone else. Afterward, you start creeping out and doing all types of fun, risky, and unforgettable things with that individual, creating an emotional experience. Soon after the female becomes pregnant, and the both of you realize that something has changed, but you both agree to do the right thing, hang in there, and be parents.

After some years of raising the child, hard financial times hit. You start borrowing money to make ends meet, you get hired and fired from jobs, and you are arguing more than having fun. Things and life have gotten real. Instead of fighting and comforting the family, you decide to leave—as if there was a choice. So you leave the child and the mother. Your reason for leaving is that this is hard and you are not happy as much anymore. You and the woman argue all the time, and you cannot keep a job. You are better off without her weighing you down, because you feel like a failure and can't handle the pressure of suffering.

The woman begs you to please stay and not to go. She says, "You have to stay and keep this family together. Things will change, and I will get another job. We can even cut out some things that we don't need." She continues begging you to please not go. "We need you, and our son needs his father. You know that he has special needs and I can't do this by myself. I need you here for our family. Please don't go, because I love you and I need you to stay."

You leave after the woman pours out her heart and expresses the dire need for you to stay and to believe things will get better. *You leave* after the cry for your help to save a wounded family member and child.

Men, I want to encourage you. Know this: You are built to comfort that hurt, not to cause the hurt. You are built to win and to take the queen home, not to use her and spit on her as if she is nothing. You are built to love the woman and support her, not tear her down as if she is not a queen. Men, you are the king, and she is the queen; and when you stand together to create a lifestyle in which both of you can rule on this earth, know that she is not for your heartbreaking games. Life is too serious, and love is the fountain of youth that preserves us from lifeless and meaningless affairs.

Men, there will always be hard times, but life is like sports; practice makes perfect, and the more you fall, the more you get up and become stronger to win. Your family is your team or platoon, and you are in charge of protecting, leading, teaching, and sharing the secret to living life in a safe awareness. Society is out to destroy the weak, raise the strong, recognize the victors, and return everyone home safely after each daily battle in life. Men of valor take on life and show grit and tenacity with their families as they weather the storms and overcome any obstacles that may be presently in the way.

Men, leaving a family is not a choice; it is a cowardly way of thinking. You have the strength to correct it and do better moving forward in the lives of your children and grandchildren. I know this because I am a man and am living the words that you are reading. That is why I am sharing this knowledge with you. Men, we are the strongest representations of our families and the first role models and superheroes that our children will know. It is also your role as a man to serve and protect your family with grit and tenacity every day that you have breath.

Be the man you were born to be and the father that you desire to be. Work at it until your vision and plan for your family become a reality and manifest themselves. Then create a cycle pipeline for your grandchildren to experience and be loved by your legacy, by putting your stake in the ground and claiming what is rightfully yours on the earth. Men, *your families are all you have.*

Be a real man of valor for yourself and your family because you were born to lead your family.

Planning Your Life

Men, having a plan is not a way to support only oneself; it is for families and the futures of children as beneficiaries. As a man, it is important to understand this information as a contributor and provider to life, inclusive of self and family. This is the priority of wisdom regarding life and preserving the future.

Men, living in this world, you need to know what you are doing and why. That means you must have an ideal and a plan for your life. For any plan to work, you must work! Nothing is given freely, and there is nothing given without a cost. Lastly, there are no free rides in this life, and if someone says there is, you had better believe that there is a hidden trick with a payback. Every person, both rich and poor, must put in the work in order to survive in this world of ambitiousness. Men, you need a plan for your life and must adhere to it until it becomes your reality. If you don't have a plan for your life, then you have planned to fail! Life has many things to offer once you move in a positive direction, but to live in this life without an idea or a plan is very difficult and is a dangerous way to live. In order to discover your value and worth, you must develop your skills and have a mental tenacity to work the plan until it manifests.

My grandfather Lawrence G. McKinley told me, "A man is only as good as his word, and his word should always be his bond to ensure good relationships in the family and with friends." He said that this is a man and told me to put away my toys and childish ways.

Men, I want to encourage you! You have the ability to change all things about yourselves. Because others can see you as important people or as lowlifes or meaningless people. Remember: people can see you only for who you are and by what you show them, which is their proof. Proof is the evidence of what you display and the legitimacy of your actions. It is very important for men to demonstrate their loyalty, build trust and respect, and practice being honest to self, family, and children. "A man is only as good as his word" and the evidence of his work. Men, with building trust, it is very important to be around on a regular basis and stand with your family through all things. Never run from problems, but embrace all things, both good and challenging, while learning from them to do better. Once again, a man is only as good as his word and actions.

Men, it is critical that you have a plan for your life, and I want to elaborate on this point as I recite a line from my first book, *The Real Enemy: The Inner Me*: *No Plan, No Progress and No Future*. Loving yourself first is the step to enlightenment!

Why is it so important for people to be positive and strive for even better? For self! One thing I know is that teenagers and adults need to be selfish about the things that are valuable and the things that will allow progress to transform them and mold them to live successfully. Personal selfishness makes a person do things for self-satisfaction, and everyone must be willing to do some things for self, because when everything and everyone is gone, you must be happy with yourself and the things you have done each day. In order to help someone else, you must first help yourself.

Never settle for just enough or for what other people give you! Why? Everyone's intentions are not in your favor; know the company that you keep. Everything done is based on trust and the relationship that is established. Make this a personal rule: only depend on your own abilities and listen to others' positive, constructive advice. Positive, constructive advice is good if it is meant to help you do something better or achieve something you have never achieved positively. Why is this a valid point? Sometimes we give our greatness away, and then we become comfortable in accepting being second best. Don't get me wrong; training is good, and you should be always willing to be trained, but you should know when the training is up. Why? After the training, there should be advancement, and it should happen within the time frame of a few years. The reason is simple: you must value your self-worth enough to want to advance yourself or you will accept crumbs off the table for less and wonder later why you did not get to the next level of advancement.

One of the keys to the reward system is to perform at your best and not let others see you sweat. Always know whom to ask for help, know when to ask for help, and never appear to have a lack of complete understanding. When you are giving your all to a situation, you are developing and activating an inward determination to persevere. This should enable you to strive to achieve goals. The acknowledgment you receive is because of what you have earned with honor and hard work. You should always reassess higher goals for yourself. Work hard and practice with the intention to become an achiever, and others will assist you in your transformation into a better performer. This mind state and ability will transfer into the required attitude to positively exist at work, complete poems, or write books; but in general, finish things you start.

Men, it is very important to have a plan to be with your families and experience the pleasure of earning and taking care of those families. Although many men know this, there are also many men who don't know this. A sad reality is that the men that do know this information change at the time of adversity due to hurt, violation by family or a loved one, or an unwanted feeling. Whichever it is, the results are bad and can become toxic, and when toxicity fills a man's heart, it confuses the mind and the man begins engaging in very risky behavior.

This is the beginning of problems and the root of lust and wasteful spending on risky desires and behaviors. The danger of this type of behavior is that it leads to further misunderstanding, misleading mental processes, and ends with a loss from the family. Its benefits support and cause separation, which can lead to being lonely and being alone in a depressed state, or being and feeling isolated. When this occurs, love is replaced with money, affection is replaced with alcohol and drugs, and attention is replaced with reckless lifestyles. Caring becomes a secondary thought and feeling and is minimized with a bad attitude about self, family, people, and life. The danger with this is that sex can become a weapon of control used to manipulate and to gain trust and material things and leave self and other empty and hurt.

This is not living responsibly or being responsible, but it is self-pleasing thinking that yields the rewards of misguidance, causing confusion and misunderstanding to others, because of your unwillingness to deal with the reality of truth, discuss the difference, and make peace and not problems. Men are born to live life with love and have family. Men, to have a family requires knowing the value of the family and having the willingness to fight for the relationship. When it is a relationship with a woman, you will have to love through it with a mind state of being the example rather than waiting on an example. Men, your families, especially the women in those families, all want and are waiting on you to set up, do well, reflect a positive image of yourself, lead, and protect them.

Men, women are always waiting on men to get serious about life, relationships, and creating homes filled with love, children, and family. Men, women are trained to be ready for love and family, and to create romantic lives filled with love and work for stable and happy lifestyles. Although a woman is very demanding at times and opinionated about her thoughts and feelings about things, it is my belief that many times she is *right* (though not all the time). Men, we have not been trained as a whole population of men to take on the responsibilities of fathering or understanding a family's needs. Most men understand what it means to be a man only through what they have seen on television or what others have told them. Most of the time, we have been directed to be unfaithful, to be abusive, to have multiple women, and to always control women. This is called playing games with people, especially when it is done in relationships while dating. The danger in this is that it can continue, and this mental state of being and unapproved conduct can be carried over into marriage as normal behavior.

Men, it is very important to learn to do the right things for your families and the ones you love. Why? Being a man means having a plan and a career to support the family's needs, spending time with family, marrying, creating a family, providing safety, providing protection, and being a voice within the family. This requires great mental discipline and willpower.

Men, we have been misinformed about how to be a man, but we can learn a new way of thinking and doing things for ourselves, our families, and our relationships. It first starts with admitting that you have not done your best at being a person, man, or father. Then you must get help through mentorship, support groups, elders in the family, or professional counseling. Men, you have the power to change and become a better you, and it matters to your manhood and family that you do so. We as a community need all men to build and protect the family, because unfortunately not all men will take this seriously or read this book.

A Man of Structure

Men, we have been fooled, and now we are paying for it! How? There are children being born in single-family homes without fathers to help raise and protect them, and these boys and girls are doing all types of unimaginable things to fill the void of improper parental guidance because of the absence of fathers. Their time is occupied and replaced by iPods, laptops, iPhones, video games, social media chats, and internet searches, which leads to mischief, crime, and immoral and unethical behaviors with the assistance of the World Wide Web. Men, you are needed in society to show that you care, to stand and protect your families from predators that lurk and dismantle the family structure. When you abandon your families, you leave room for them to be infiltrated. This is not necessary, and it has a cost. It is time to understand the error of our ways in the form of lack of commitment and the inability to endure the pain that every family encounters. Family crisis is a part of growth, and there will be love and pain.

Men, what if women left every time a crisis arose or when they had differences? Where would your families be today? Probably lost and worse off! Women have maintained families for years, but the fact of the matter is that it takes a village to raise a family, and when a person, especially a male, is not present, then the family can be easily dismantled, and it is left vulnerable (because a male is the protector and the watchman, and the practice of rites of passage will reinforce this point).

Men, every time that you are not around the family on a daily, weekly, monthly, and annual basis, the family is weakened. It is time to stop running from problems and know that problems will always be around forever in all relationships. The object is not to focus on the problems but to come up with answers inclusively.

Look for positive solutions that ignite love and togetherness. There is a saying that goes, "Boys play with toys and play games." If this is true of you, I want to encourage you to stop it *now*. It is time to change how you see relationships and then step up and do the right thing for yourself and your family. It's time to cultivate your family by engaging in family-oriented events and planning them with other family members. The family should always think about the future and discuss the progress of the children while emphasizing the importance of them doing well. How things go in the family does matter, and together families do not have to suffer; they can instead accomplish things with respect and love. This requires leadership and the ability to cultivate your family on a regular basis with an intention to discuss family matters.

Ten Steps of Rites of Passage

According to Charles Lee-Johnson, CEO of the National Family and Education Center, who wrote the Ten Step Rites of Passage, the ten steps that one must master to live are

1. personal rites,
2. emotional rites,
3. spiritual rites,
4. mental rites,
5. social rites,
6. political rites,
7. economical rites,
8. historical rites,
9. culture rites, and
10. physical rites.

He states, " ...these rites of passage is a response to the need for programs for teen fathers in 1985, Mr. Johnson realized that most boys are not prepared for adulthood or fatherhood ... so before teen fathers can learn to be a father, they must first be taught how to be men, because boys can't be fathers, only men can be fathers."

Men, wake up! Women and society need you to lead and be men!

The Problem Solver

A mother is a single parent who must feed the children. When a man leaves his family or the child's mother, he becomes a single man. These statements are false; they are lies. The status is the same for both, and both should continue be responsible for feeding their children daily.

Men, wake up! Being a problem-solver does not mean being a dictator or the boss over someone. It means that you have the ability to make decisions alone or with others. We all have opinions, and it is only fair that everyone's voices is heard and respected. Men, you are needed for your ability to fix things that are broken, but just doing your part is not enough. In this life, being able to coexist is very important when it comes to the family unit. It is hard for individuals, so it is very important to do things corporately with your family as one unit. Doing so requires more effort than normal, because as a man, you should want to carry more responsibilities than everyone else in your family, especially as a husband or father. Leaving your family because of differences does not make you a person of concern, but it can be seen as an embarrassment to the circle of life, men and manhood, and, more so, to your family.

Although most problems are caused by two people, when you don't admit to your part of the problem, you are wrong on so many levels of the relationship. In most relationships, this is the cause of the problem. Not being honest is the same as not being considerate. I learned that for those men that are responsible, there is more to do, because no matter what good we do, when a man is not present in a child's life at home or involved with his family and the needs of his family, there is a loss. Men, the words that I am saying are not negative but should be accepted as a voice of brotherhood and positive motivation expressing that your availability is needed by your family and society.

My intention for writing this book and to say what I am saying is only to awaken the greatness in men and to address the need for more men to be present. There is a dire need for men to do better as it pertains to these matters of the heart, especially for children in the family, the family unit, and society. Don't believe the hype that men are not needed or wanted. Although a lot of people, both men and women, believe this statement, they are speaking from a hurt place of absenteeism of their fathers in their lives or from being hurt and left broken-hearted, or both.

Men, we sometimes use the excuse that we did not have fathers to show us things, and although this can be true, don't let this experience overshadow the fact that you can do better than your fathers. Men have used this truth as a disability, and I do understand this, because I thought like this too, but now I know better, and I am sharing it with you. I learned that sometimes you just need to do what was not done for you, because you know it needs to be done or someone advised you to do it.

Men, know this: many girls, sisters, and ladies did not have fathers to raise and protect them or give them guidance either. Our mothers raised us with the best that they had to give based on their understanding of how to raise a child, and they were not perfect, but those that were there were there, and they never gave up or ran from the responsibility. Many of them, too, were fatherless, and they pushed on for many years and made many sacrifices that will never be revealed; and they did it for their children and the family. Men, when you get a good, not perfect, woman, and she is talking positivity, you need to listen to her, especially if she is inspiring you to do more to better yourself. Let the ego go, be grateful, and take up your role as a male provider in addition to the woman. Take on and carry more responsibility for the family for self-gratification and to be a man in a family. Family is very imperfect, so don't look for any type of perfectness, but build the family by striving to be a family that stays together.

Never do things or think things with a negative or painful mind state. In all things, act out of love. Watch the negativity that sometimes prevents men from doing right, but do the opposite and do what you wish was done for you to help your family and be a better person and a better man. Men, our roles as men, leaders, husbands, and fathers are so important because we protect and provide, and without us, our families become vulnerable prey.

If there is no man in the home to protect the mother and children, then who will do it? When you decided to leave because you could not endure the challenges of the home dynamics and a woman, you were not acting maturely, and you lacked the ability to endure the challenges that life threw at you. I want to correct this error of the mind and encourage you. When a man marries a woman and they have children, things change. Know that you were born to be a man to lead and protect your family. Did you ever stop to think and ask why these challenges happened? I want to give you my answer of encouragement. It happened because it was meant for you to learn how to endure and to overcome, because this is a weak area that you need to work on to be a man of valor who endures until the end of life.

Men, when we are always challenged with something in a relationship that we need to work on, it is our challenge, so we must take accountability and responsibility, and be empowered to know that we can overcome these things ourselves. No other person is entitled to change to make you feel better; you do the work to change because you want to be a better person.

Men, know this: you have the power to change and influence your family, but you must demonstrate and endure, which will show off your intent to love your family unconditionally. Family love is everything to a family unit, and the challenges will be present within the family and are meant to be solved together. The challenges that are presented are for all members to consider changing for the bettering of the relationship and to be on the same page. Challenges are not designed to cause separation; they are designed for correction and to get everyone to be of the same accord with others.

Why is this important? Because it is necessary to improve your character and your ability to love and stay in relationships. As men and fathers, we have learned this for self, and that is why I am writing this to you—because I realized that this knowledge is needed for me to change inwardly and to be able to do my part. But instead I ran and left my family, looking foolish, and it broke my trust with my family. Men, we are born to endure with grit and tenacity, and there is nothing that can't be done when men put their minds to it. Have a focus point and set your mind on it, because it is family and it is the right thing to do.

Men, it is critical to know that when you decide to leave a family or marriage with children, you leave behind a broken-hearted situation and a broken home. Leaving is a choice, and I want you to know the impact of your decision. Accept what you have done. It does not matter what the woman did to push you away, whether she did not believe in you, or whether you wanted to be free. Whatever the situation is does matter, but what also matters is that you belong to a family and there are children attached to you as family, perhaps biologically.

It is your responsibility as a man to be there for your family, and you must do your best to find a way to make it work together. Working together is important, and if you want something to work, you must work on it. To get gainful results requires patience and time as you wait for the manifestation of the work that you put in it over a period of time. If you, as a man, don't learn to do well today for a better tomorrow, you will continue to destroy the hopes and dreams of a young lady and children, and prevent a family from seeing their son, brother, husband, and friend do well. You desire better for yourself and the family.

Being a man is something that is genetically given at the time of birth, and being a man is hard. Being a father is a challenge and should challenge your life forever because we should want to be in our children's lives and forever learn how to endure and love. It was not easy for me, but I endured and made many attempts to be there and remembered to always be there for the family. I am thankful for having a changed mind; it is a blessing to me and my life to be able to be a blessing to you and write this book.

Change in Status—Man to Father

As a man, it is important that you are preparing to be a father. Why? As a man, when you have a son or daughter, the child is waiting to meet his or her mother and father when he or she is born. As the child grows up, he or she will want more of your time, interaction, and engagement in his or her life.

Time matters, because parenting is a 24-7, 365-day-a-year responsibility.

A good mother is designed to raise a child. She has the children and usually has the most interaction with the children when it comes to taking care of them. Even when she is sick, is not feeling well, or is on vacation, she can do these things, because she is a parent. But this does not give the father an out. The children need both parents, and when one parent is gone all the time, the other parent is putting in the work and the children are being taught from one personal perspective.

Parenting is a 24-7 task, and it requires being in a child's life and being present. Men, picking up your children biweekly or when you can is not being a full-time parent. Picking up your children during the week and weekends, paying for activities, going on field trips, and assisting with homework is being a full-time father. The mother needs a break and desires a break, just as you do. Men, if your children's mother has the children and is struggling daily but making it anyway, stop making it harder for her and relieve her. Why? The child is yours too. Just because you work and make the money and the mother is not living in the same house, that does not give you a pass on being a parent in the children's lives. The children have two parents, and it is a shared responsibility. It takes two people to create the child, and it takes two people to raise the child. As men, this is what we do as leaders, and you should be happy and should hope that all things work out so the mother and family are proud of you for doing well for your children. Men, knowing this information about the importance of you being a father to the children is impressive, and there is joy in knowing that you are needed. This is a great thought! What better opportunity for a man to do well for his children and family. Now that you know this, if you have not done this for your family, this would be a great time to right some wrongs. You can be the man or king that you were born to be and the man you soulfully desire to be.

What about the mother that tricked you, lied to you, and got pregnant when you didn't want any children? This is a challenging situation, and if you are in doubt, get a blood test to relieve your mind so you can raise your child. If you know and claim the child, then deal with your hurt but raise that child. The child is innocent, and it is the parental relationship that deserve t be work on with forgiveness.

Let's clear the air and remove the games. If you don't want children, there are four things you can do to prevent fatherhood:

1. Don't have sex with anyone.
2. Use a condom at all times.
3. If you're sure you won't want any children in the future, get a vasectomy.
4. If she says that she can't have any children, check the paperwork. Better yet, don't have sex.

The greatest way to prevent having unwanted children is to abstain from sex until marriage. Why? It is a tough pill to swallow, and having children you don't want can be altered by protected or no sex . Women lie to get what they want, and men do too, but in this case prevention is simple: protect yourself at all costs or abstain from sexual activities. It's hard, but the bigger picture is that an unwanted child did not ask to be here. So pick up the child and love the child despite the mother's and your differences. If the child is yours, then act like it and be a father so the child can see a positive role model, and you will be the child's first hero. The child's first heroes are the mother and father, so don't tarnish the vision that the child has of you. This should give you comfort in knowing that you're a hero to your children and that you are able to make a great impact whether you had a father or mother in your life or not.

This is a positive opportunity and a chance to ensure that your children don't encounter the same bad and lonely feeling that you did. You should be more empowered to do the opposite of what was done to you, because being a parent is not easy and is a rite of passage within itself. It is the transition from being a single man to fatherhood. That is why it is important to read this book to gain a better understanding about your need and purpose in life as a valued person.

Being a father is the greatest gift that a man could ever receive and be entrusted with as a responsible parent who gives guidance to a child or children. It is also a responsibility that is an honor to accept. Why? Life is the greatest gift, whether the children have your genes or the genes from your wife or girlfriend. Children are children, and family is family! Men, this information is designed to cause an awakening within you that will cause you to open your eyes and mind to the highest understanding about life and to give relief and positive energy to being a parent. Your role as a father is to demonstrate love and discipline with understanding and a loving heart.

Men, it is imperative that you learn the value of yourself and family, and that you plan for your manhood. Planning your life should be as important as being a productive citizen. Men, if you know this but have not done it, that is okay. It's never too late to do it now. You should want to do it, because it is the right and respectable thing to do. One of the most difficult things that I have experienced as a teacher was when I heard one of the mothers during a teacher conference explain why she thought her son acted up by stating that his father lied, never came around, and was always breaking her son's heart. Men, please don't be the reason why your child's mother and family cry about you because of what you have not done as a father. Men, you should be doing things to make the family smile, because you make their day when you are around. Men, you are valuable sources, and you are needed as peacemakers. Men, wake up!

Being a Leader

As a man, it is important that you are mentally prepared to be a father and leader. Why? It is your role to ensure that your children are led specifically by *you*. If you have children, it is up to you to teach them about life. Remember: if you don't raise and train your children to go the right way and to be productive citizens, you, as a father, have failed too. You have a direct impact and influence on your child's life, and if you don't support your child, then you have let that child down, the mother down, the family down, and the future down. But it is not too late to do the right thing and to believe that you can change for the betterment of yours and those who need you.

Your leadership is imperative. That is why this book is very important for you to read and reread several times as you internalize, do the work, and share it with others. I believe that I was inspired to write this book to give knowledge to men that will wake them up about the importance of being available for their families. I have provided an example of a leadership chart, and it is my hope that the chart will allow you, the reader, to examine yourself based on your leadership style. I also want to encourage you to research the different leadership styles. Why? The type of leader you are will determine the impact you will have. If you know your leadership style, then it should inspire you and in time manifest in your intention to live life as a leader.

If you don't know your leadership style, this gives you the opportunity to pick your style and strive to become the man you want to be.

So look at the example chart and think about the ideal leader that you are, and add to your character with new information for you to strive for in the future. Your leadership abilities are part of your personality traits, your thoughts, your habits, and how you react to others. Personality traits are the distinguishing characteristics or qualities of a person. It is known to be the trend of actions, outlook, feelings, and habits regarding specific things, situations, and people. Choose your leadership style, and strive to become that leader.

Leadership: theory and practice.[1]

Leadership Chart

Leadership Theories:	Strenghts:	Weaknesses:	Personal Reaction
Path-Goal Theory	Using a Path Goal Theory approach to leadership has several positive features. Firstly, this theory attempts to incorporate the motivation principles of the expectancy theory and second its model is practical and easy to use.	Although there are several positive aspect of Path-Goal Theory, it fail to explain the different roles of leaders and managers. The time constraints to effectively deploys very narrow.	Although in an attempt to clearly visualize the visions, I sometimes get caught up in the overall progress and save little time to consider the individual.

[1] Northouse, P. G. (2001). Leadership: theory and practice. Thousand Oaks, California: Sage Publications.

Implication for:

Self	Team	Organization	Culture
In order to employ this approach effectively, it would be helpful to create a questionnaire for staff, in order to uncover some of their motivators. Communication between myself and team members is vital for success.	Teams are strong because they know what the goal is and have a clear roadmap to accomplish the mission.	The theory allows for building. Teams goals become departmental goals, departmental goals become organization goals. For the organization this theory helps push forwad organizational initiatives.	The culture of the organization when using the path-goal theory suggest the motivation of employees is a strategic direction, and is a used as a method for production.

After reviewing the chart, you should see some of the traits that identify you or that you desire as a leader, so develop a plan on how you can become that leader. Men, it is time for a mental change, and you don't have forever to do it. Yes, it takes time to develop, but you can take action steps daily. It is very important to invest in yourself. Men, wake up!

Being a kindhearted and fair man that your family members can look up to, rely on, and be proud of is a great thought. That role is waiting on you to fill it daily, and it is a choice. Although all people have a choice in life to do and not do things, this conditional thought was not shown to a lot of men. This thought can be a reality if you strive for it, but it won't be a perfect situation, because there is no perfect situation without flaws. So if you messed up in the past and you are concerned about how your family will look at you, don't worry, because they will look at you strangely and not trust you if have not done what you need to do to be a part of your family and demonstrate love and ask for forgiveness.

So step up today and make a difference. The past is gone and over.

Today and moving forward is what matters, and yesterday is gone, so don't judge yourself so harshly because you did not do your best, but see this as a positive opportunity to get it right, and do something to prove yourself each day. Your loyalty must be proven, and this is not hard, but it does take commitment and dedication. It also takes a mental willingness to handle the backlash from and acceptance of your past offenses. Remember: relationships are not perfect! This statement implies that there will be work that has to be done and that all things are considered to be fair. The secret is having, speaking, and thinking the intent to love through it all.

Men, all people must learn from their pasts of wrongful behavior and do better jobs at not repeating it over and over, but you should never walk out on your family. We all will fall short on pleasing each other, but we must learn not to do it again. Why? Because it is very important for you to set your mind free from this lie and move forward with the impetus to overcome, while breaking this curse in your mind that is filled with bad information about parenting and how men should father.

This is critical, because there is no shortcut to parenting and there are no breaks in family problems, but there are breakups because of the lack of integrity. Men, as protectors, it will be your integrity that holds your families together no matter what, and you choosing to stay and work it out is a blessing. A true role model with understanding about family is not perfect but can stand and stay.

Men, remember that your role is to serve and protect your families at all cost. When you don't communication and go out and waste money, drink, smoke, and cheat, you are doing everyone a disservice. Remember: women can do the same thing, because they, too, need a break and get frustrated. However, they stay focused on the children and remain in the home. But when you are not focused on family affairs, then anything can happen to distract you and pull you away from your family values.

Parenting and being a family man can be hard, but the payoff is worthy of your time invested into your family. Live a life filled with planning and communication with your family, and strive to create opportunity that yield a good return. Parenting in a relationship or as a single parent is the same responsibility. Men, this is the best news ever, because you are needed, and your assistance is warranted. When you are involved with family, you are also being a leader within your family. Men, remember to make sure that there are family gatherings, and join in the responsibility of creating family unity as often as you can. The family unit will demonstrate and share family unity out of love and not for selfish gain of attention.

You Are Born to Lead

Men, innately there is a burning desire to make things work, and sometimes it's hard to communicate this. For this desire to be activated, and to achieve excellence, you have to fight and have a goal to be in a family. This means reeducating oneself in order to gain a better understanding about self and life. It also means discovering the leader that lies dormant within, hidden behind hurtful encounters, harsh communications, unforgiving situations, criticism, and financial difficulties. Men, I want to be transparent about what I just said, because as a man I know it is a very sensitive conversation, and I will be direct about it.

This lack of communication is part of life, and every person that lives in this world will have to experience it, but it takes a strong-willed attitude for you to stand and demonstrate grit, tenacity, desire, and the willingness to prove that you love yourself, family, and life. If this is lack of communication doesn't change, this will continue throughout your life until death do you part from this world. Each time this challenge comes and goes, it is not to derail you, but it is a test of your development that is intended to enable and prepare you to lead. We all are born to lead in the area of our passion, and this is revealed in our lifestyles.

Men, you can do anything that you put your mind to. As a man, I have learned that there will be and must be public humiliation with criticism. Why? In my opinion, to see you fall because of bad choices that need correction and then to see you change for the better is a change that is great. Life is ever changing, and you must mature and evolve as you endure in all your relationships in life. Life is not easy, but with a plan you can alleviate certain pitfalls. Without a plan, it will be harder for your life and your dreams and aspirations to manifest.

True leadership and responsible victories come from perseverance. This commitment will raise your level of leadership and provide a vision of how to be a positive reflection. Don't be afraid to fail, because failures empower you to do things better without the risks. Men, your families are what your lives should be about when it comes to the future. The future is part of the leading force to ensure that your leadership and victories happens and that there is a promising tomorrow.

Men, no one wants you to leave. Your families want to be able to rely on your presence, your emotional support, your love and your financial assistance.

As a man, you have more power and influence than you probably know, and all you have to do is show up. Start talking about family investments to bring about unity, and watch the elders ask a lot of questions. Once they are confident in what you are saying, they will support you, but don't play with family business and money. If you do, then you will kill their trust in you.

Men, the trust you build is the trust that is earned. Let all that you do be a reflection of your intent and love that you want to have for your families, even if not for you. Your love can change them. All families are dysfunctional and need a strong person to secure their confidence and the future.

There are many pairs of eyes that are watching and waiting on your great inspiration to show up to show them the way to a better place.

Men, you have activated the desire to overcome the obstacles and beat the odds that life will afford for you to encounter for personal growth. The obstacles and challenges must happen for you to learn how to do things better the next time. Practice makes it better, and as a man, you can master your leadership in your family and in your career, but they both require practice for you to reach the desired result. Practice every day until a wealth of knowledge and financial gain showers down upon you and covers your family as beneficiaries of your endeavors. Share ideas with the family and develop a family plan inclusively. If no one wants to, do it anyway, because the family will benefit from it in the future. Never second-guess doing something for the family.

Personal Development

Men, it is very important that you attend some personal development seminars or classes. Our present thoughts must have self-control and personal development along with the assurance that mentally you have a direction and purpose. Personal development assists with customizing your effective goals, which inspire and motivate you to stay focused until you achieve success. Setting your personal development goals allows you time and commitment to invest in your greatest human capital—you. Another way to look at personal development is as caring for yourself and ensuring that you are developing yourself and becoming a mature man because you want the rewards of doing so. In all things that you do, let the reflection of the immeasurable amount of love and the standard that you have for yourself as a man speak for you!

There are ten benefits of personal development that a man should be proud to learn, know, and demonstrate:

1. A sense of direction-making decisions and knowing when to ask for help to reduce risks
2. Being focused and effective—knowing your weakness and strengths, and developing them to resist distraction
3. Being motivated—knowing that the end goal and the purpose of the dream is to get it done
4. Being resilient—dealing with challenges with confidence to know that doing so is a part of the human process
5. Having family values—doing things to support your family
6. Networking and relationship building, which cultivates long-lasting relationships, and choosing friends wisely
7. Planning for the future—doing positive things to improve and be effective and result-driven
8. Being ready to die and believing in yourself to strive to overcome and be a changed positive man
9. Having self-awareness—knowing who you are
10. Visionary-insight about the quality of life for self and family

We are have both good and bad characteristics, but you, as an individual, are able to choose which characteristics best define who you are as a human being.

CHAPTER FOUR

FATHERHOOD

I have listed some alarming statistics about the state of crisis concerning men and the need for them to step up to be a part of their families. If problems and dark secrets exist within your family, I urge you to address them. Why? Because your family has a need to be protected and loved by you. This is what you were born to do as a male, a son, a brother, an uncle, a grandfather, a father, an elder, and a mature man with responsibility.

The Statistical Facts are from the Fatherless Generation Article2

Statistics

- "63% of youth suicides are committed by youths from fatherless homes (US Department of Health / US Census Bureau)—5 times the overall average.
- 90% of all homeless and runaway children are from fatherless homes—32 times the overall average.

---

² Sabrina. "Statistics." Fatherless Generation (blog). https://thefatherlessgeneration. wordpress.com/statistics/.

- 85% of all children who show behavior disorders come from fatherless homes—20 times the overall average. (US Centers for Disease Control)
- 80% of rapists with anger problems come from fatherless homes—14 times the overall average. (*Justice & Behavior* 14, 403–26)
- 71% of all high school dropouts come from fatherless homes—9 times the overall average. (National Principals Association report)

The Father Factor in Education

- Fatherless children are twice as likely to drop out of school.
- Children with fathers who are involved in their lives are 40% less likely to repeat a grade in school.
- Children with fathers who are involved in their lives are 70% less likely to drop out of school.
- Children with fathers who are involved in their lives are more likely to get As in school.
- Children with fathers who are involved in their lives are more likely to enjoy school and engage in extracurricular activities.
- 75% of all adolescent patients in chemical abuse centers come from fatherless homes—10 times the overall average.

The Father Factor in Drug and Alcohol Abuse

Researchers at Columbia University found that children living in two-parent households with poor relationships with their fathers were 68% more likely to smoke, drink, or use drugs compared to all teens in two-parent households. Teens in single-mother households are at a 30% higher risk than those in two-parent households.

- 70% of youths in state-operated institutions come from fatherless homes—9 times the overall average. (US Department of Justice, September 1988)

- 85% of all youths in prison come from fatherless homes—20 times the average. (Fulton Co., Georgia, Texas Department of Correction)

The Father Factor in Incarceration

Even after controlling for income, youths in father-absent households still had significantly higher odds of incarceration than those in mother–father families. Youths who never had a father in the household experienced the highest odds. A 2002 Department of Justice survey of 7,000 inmates revealed that 39% of jail inmates lived in mother-only households. Approximately 46% of jail inmates in 2002 had a previously incarcerated family member. One-fifth had experienced a father in prison or jail.

The Father Factor in Crime

A study of 109 juvenile offenders indicated that family structure significantly predicts delinquency. Adolescents, particularly boys, in single-parent families were at higher risk of status, property, and person delinquencies. Moreover, students attending schools with a high proportion of children of single parents are also at risk. A study of 13,986 women in prison showed that more than half grew up without their father. 42% grew up in a single-mother household, and 16% lived with neither parent.

The Father Factor in Child Abuse

- Compared to living with both parents, living in a single-parent home doubles the risk that a child will suffer physical, emotional, or educational neglect. The overall rate of child abuse and neglect in single-parent households is 27.3 children per 1,000, whereas the rate of overall maltreatment in two-parent households is 15.5 per 1,000.

- Daughters of single parents without a father involved are 53% more likely to marry as teenagers, 711% more likely to have children as teenagers, 164% more likely to have a premarital birth, and 92% more likely to get divorced themselves.
- Adolescent girls raised in two-parent homes with involved fathers are significantly less likely to be sexually active than girls raised without involved fathers.
- 43% of US children live without their fathers. (US Census Bureau)
- 90% of homeless and runaway children are from fatherless homes. (US DHHS, US Census Bureau)
- 80% of rapists motivated with displaced anger come from fatherless homes. (*Criminal Justice & Behavior* 14, 403–26, 1978)
- 71% of pregnant teenagers lack a father. (US Department of Health and Human Services press release, Friday, March 26, 1999)
- 63% of youth suicides are committed by youths from fatherless homes. (US DHHS, US Census Bureau)
- 85% of children who exhibit behavioral disorders come from fatherless homes. (US Centers for Disease Control)
- 90% of adolescent repeat arsonists live with only their mothers.[3]
- 71% of high school dropouts come from fatherless homes. (National Principals Association Report on the State of High Schools)
- 75% of adolescent patients in chemical abuse centers come from fatherless homes. (Rainbows for All God's Children)
- 70% of juveniles in state-operated institutions have no father. (US Department of Justice, Special Report, September 1988)
- 85% of youths in prisons grew up in a fatherless home. (Fulton County Georgia jail populations, Texas Department of Corrections, 1992)
- Fatherless boys and girls are twice as likely to drop out of high school, twice as likely to end up in jail, and four times more likely to need help for emotional or behavioral problems. (US DHHS news release, March 26, 1999)

---

[3] Wray Herbert, "Dousing the Kindlers," *Psychology Today*, January 1985, 28.

- The responsible fatherhood research literature generally supports the claim that a loving and nurturing father improves outcomes for children, families, and communities.
- Children with involved, loving fathers are significantly more likely to do well in school, have healthy self-esteem, exhibit empathy and prosocial behavior, and avoid high-risk behaviors, such as drug use, truancy, and criminal activity, compared to children who have uninvolved fathers.
- Studies on parent–child relationships and child well-being show that fatherly love is an important factor in predicting the social, emotional, and cognitive development and functioning of children and young adults.
- 24 million children (34 %) live absent their biological father.
- Nearly 20 million children (27%) live in single-parent homes.
- 43% of first marriages dissolve within fifteen years; about 60 percent of divorcing couples have children, and approximately one million children each year experience the divorce of their parents.
- Fathers who live with their children are more likely to have a close, enduring relationship with their children than those who do not.
- Compared to children born within marriage, children born to cohabiting parents are three times as likely to experience father absence, and children born to unmarried, noncohabiting parents are four times as likely to live in a father-absent home.
- About 40 percent of children in father-absent homes have not seen their fathers at all during the past year, 26 percent of absent fathers live in different states than their children, and 50 percent of children living absent their fathers have never set foot in their fathers' homes.
- Children who live absent their biological fathers are, on average, at least two to three times more likely to be poor; to use drugs; to experience educational, health, emotional and behavioral problems; to be victims of child abuse; and to engage in criminal behavior than their peers who live with their married biological or adoptive parents.

- From 1995 to 2000, the proportion of children living in single-parent homes slightly declined, while the proportion of children living with two married parents remained stable."

Fathers

A soldier's mission is to serve, protect, and educate for the great good of his or her nation. A father's nation is his family. A soldier's motto is to leave no soldier behind, so leave no family member behind.

A father is more than just a sperm that fertilizes an egg. He is a male that transitions into an adult man. That adult man then seeks to be in a marital relationship with a woman, and they produce children, plan or unplanned, together. Any man can impregnate a woman, but a father is willing to stay and care for his family. An involved father, called a dad, assumes the responsibility of being a provider. In some situations, an adult male marries into a ready-made family and assumes the responsibility of raising children that are not his. A father is a father in both cases.

Men who are not serious about relationships tend to jump in and out of relationships for self- gratification, and this may cause problems with women, because most, if not all, women want to be in serious relationships with the intent of getting married. Therefore, a man should want to be responsible in every relationship and not have a mentality of freeloading and pray on women for selfish reasons. Men, know your role. Stop the game-playing and be the good man and father that a woman is looking for.

When you look into your child's eyes, you should see a reflection of yourself, and it should touch your soul. You should also know that his or her future is promising because you are the child's father. Men, even if you are in a ready-made family, you should still be able see a bright future in a child because of who you are and the fatherhood that you bring. Men, know that all children are a blessing and that you are the father of a nation.

A father will love his children unconditionally through good times and bad times. Societal woes regarding young males and females and their questionable behavior come into play through the choices being made as a result of a lack of influence from their parents, specifically fathers. Just as young adults have influences that may deter them, men are under the same influences, just on a higher plane. Men, we must stop prioritizing the use of drugs and alcohol over being family men and fathers. This behavior causes lack of esteem and responsibility in the family, and some of this type of behavior can inhibit the ability to do anything. The correct mind state and behavior is to know that you are needed in your family. A father must have the courage and tenacity to address situations with his children as they grow and become young adults. It is the father's responsibility to instill truth, love, and honesty. In all situations, be a man that yields to be a listener and who will monitor his children's behaviors while accepting their differences. You must find a way to still love your children and let them live life through their mistakes with truth and love. Parenting is an act of unconditional love. Why? Because no one who has ever lived has been perfect.

Men, this is the greatest opportunity for you to do well and not be judged. You will be praised by your wife's and your child's mother, family, and friends. However, there will be challenges and imperfect situations that you will have to learn from in order to make corrections. Even though your family will be vocal out of concern, you should still stand up and take your place in your family.

Being a father is like being trusted with the hearts of others. You are the core that stabilizes emotions and ensures that everyone is doing well. You are the caretaker of balancing, and you are the disciplinarian. You are needed as the contributor to establish in your family and your children the cognitive, language, social development, and academic skills that ensure progress. You are the strength of building a strong inner core within the family unit, creating a sense of well-being and good health. You are the builder of confidence, competitiveness, and self-esteem with the entire family as you encourage them to be authentic to being themselves. You are a leader of influence in your family and your relationships. As a father, your children and their mother are your primary responsibility, and you should be proud of this opportunity to make a first impression while making a difference in the family. You are the leader!

Because of your demonstration as a leader, everyone will reap from your hard work, intelligence, and support. How you engage and cultivate will determine how effective you are in your relationships. But do not use timetables and have expectations for instant turnarounds. It may be something you've done in the past that needs to redeem you, or maybe not, but everyone needs time to process new changes. Everyone was not thinking about your great idea and may not be ready for it, because you can't build a family foundation in a day.

Fathers are aware of the needs of their families, knowing that they are models that everyone looks to. Your daughter will look for men who have the same patterns and behavior that you have. So if you present love and kindness, she will search out the same.

Boys, on the other hand, look for fathers to be role models they can emulate. Boys look for fatherly approval in everything they do and copy fatherly behaviors. Fathers, your sons will be the same type of man that you show them. If you are abusive, controlling, and dominating, these character traits will imprint the patterns of your sons' lives as they mature. So the way a father behaves toward his children is the way they will behave toward their children. With positive behavior from you, your children with reproduce what you've shown them.

The heart of fatherhood is understanding the following: anyone can create a baby, but being a father takes a lifetime and is something that you will practice every day for the remainder of your life. Men, your role as a father should be to demonstrate care and love to all your children; even if those children are not yours biologically, the same care and love must be shown. Your impact on the children's lives will help shape them into the people they will become.

Fathers, you also have to be considerate for your children's mothers. The mother is family and is a pillar in the development of a child's emotional well-being and the core of the family. Children look to their parents to be in their lives for love and care. Men, remember this: fathers are responsible for enforcing the rules and the law of character. All rely on fathers to provide a feeling of security, both physical and emotional. Children want to make their fathers proud, but an involved father promotes inner growth and strength.

Studies have shown that when fathers are affectionate and supportive, it greatly affects a child's cognitive and social development. It also instills an overall sense of well-being and self-confidence. Fathers set the standards for families, and mothers offer a reinforcing push with love. Please realize that your presence is needed daily. Why? Your children's futures depends on it! Being a father is a lifelong commitment, and you are the strongest influence to support your children as they grow older. Therefore, it is important to treat the mother and children with respect, love, and kindheartedness. Remember that their perceptions of you come through thoughts and patterns that you have shown them, either good or bad. That is why it is important for fathers to set great relationships with mothers and children; it determines how they relate to others.

Men, wake up! Your children and family are relying on you to father and lead them with love and guidance. Alert: the statement "A woman doesn't need a man" is infesting the minds of the female population. The reason this is so relevant is because men are not around to prove otherwise. Children have watched their single mothers endure rough times. If you are not staying or helping financially, then you are part of the problem. Shortcomings are not welcome, and women are moving on without men.

Fathers, your number-one fan, follower, inspiration and teammate is your children! As I stated earlier, your sons will model your behavior and character. It is important to know that they will seek your approval. Why is this important to know? We don't understand the depth of this responsibility or the action steps it takes to be a good father and role model. As human beings, we all grow up looking for a hero to imitate. That hero is *you!* If you, as a father, are absent but present, your son will seek approval of other male figures to fill this void, and, also be mindful that they may be influenced to model after theirs mother or other females because of your absent. This is one reason why some boys are displaying more feminine behavior.

Teaching your son the aspects of manhood will help him to survive in a world when he feels lost and has no love. In turn, he will blame himself, thinking it is his fault because his father left. Fathers, wake up!

Men, wake up! Your children and family are relying on you to father and lead them with love and guidance.

A man has to be stable for his family, and the mother creates the foundation of the family. It is my belief that when men understand the importance of fatherhood, men will do better. Fatherhood is when a man can cultivate his family with love, responsibility, respect, and forgiveness. For that to happen, the father must be in love with his wife, children, and family. A man will experience many encounters, insults, pain, and tyranny, but he must learn not to let life's challenges get the best of him or break his spirit. Keep your determination, but continue to love yourself, your family, and living. A man must have self-control and omnidirectional goodness of his being and communication if he needs help to accomplish a desired goal.

According to M. Scott Peck, MD, the author of *The Road Less Traveled*, "to be free people we must assume total responsibility for themselves, but in doing so must possess the capacity to reject responsibility that is not truly ours. To be organized and efficient, to live wisely, we must daily delay gratification and keeping an eye on the future; yes, to live joyously we must also possess the capacity, when it is not distractive, to live in the present and act spontaneously. In other words, discipline itself must be disciplined. The art of discipline required to discipline is what I call balancing."

Being a man is much different from being a father, although they are one and the same. This is what fatherhood inclusively defines. It is my belief that men have an innate ability to be fathers. This ability is built up and fights to be manifested as the male grows in responsibilities. The more you learn, the more you will implement throughout life. It is very important that all males realize that the inner man wants to become king. Being king occurs when you possess things, not people, while ensuring the education and well-being of your family. Being a father is the highest responsibility ever bestowed upon a man. It requires love, harmony, and beauty. I will elaborate: the love of father is a sign of strength, patience, submission to understanding, listening, and being supportive.

The harmony of the father creates a sense of serenity, joy, love, and care. You must be aware of things trying to infiltrate, divide, destroy, and kill any aspect of your family that causes pain. The beauty of being a father is demonstrating strength and a shoulder for the family to rest on during the tough times, disenchanting times, and financial hardships. A father has to see the beauty of his staying to weather these storms, to uplift when praises are needed, and to make solid, sound decisions to ensure the security of the future of the family. This comes through love instilled through family gatherings, vacations, church/inspirational moments, and travel.

Being a father is not paying child support alone; it means being present and participating in ongoing affairs and recreational entertainment. There is no solid future without a father, but that does not mean that the child and the mother cannot move on. The father is the example of support of the child's logic and emotion about the importance of life. It is also the example of overcoming trying times, enjoying great times, and knowing when to spend and to when to save for hard times.

Fatherhood teaches a father's role as being able to work, to inspire, and to love. Why? These are always needed by the family, and especially by the children. A father is the first male role model that every child meets, and it is so imperative that fathers are there for their children, because children depend on their fathers to determine and set the precedent.

Men, wake up! The need for fatherhood is imperative to the family. Without a father present, the family becomes imbalanced.

Being a father is a statement that says you are needed by family—the mother and children. This is a *fact* whether you are together or not. Your responsibility as a man and a father is to serve and protect the family at all costs. This is what you need to know in your role as a man and father despite the differences and problems that you and the mother are having. When children are born, they are innocent. A child is born to two parents, planned or unplanned, in the midst of both having unprotected fun. Now it is time to step up and care for the newborn that resulted from that fun. Men, wake up! You were born to be fathers, and you should be pleased and happy. Why? Because there are some couples and individuals that cannot have children, and they would die to be called parents.

Men, you are the protectors of your children and so are their mothers. It is your role, and this should bring you pleasure in knowing that they are safe and taken care of by you. As a man and a father, you should be excited that you have the opportunity to cover your family for the rest of your life. To be the caretaker over another human being is the greatest responsibility that you will ever experience, and it will change your life forever. All the money and material things in the world will never add up to the value of a human being or family. Family is a gift to the world now and for the future.

My child's father,

I know we have our differences in our opinions, but we have to do better in our communication, especially when it comes to the concern of our daughter. I know you love our daughter, and that is a fact.

I am writing because I know what kind of man you are as a father and the love you have for her as your angel. Your daughter is growing up, and she is very aware of things and her mind never stops going. She is formulating her own opinion about your absence. She has expressed that she does not feel loved by you and she doesn't think that you care about her or love her. Her reason is that you have a new family now. Every day you call and text stating that you are coming to pick her up, and she literally sits by the window, staring and waiting on your arrival with excitement to see you. When she gets tired of waiting, she goes to bed, closes the door, and cries herself to sleep with no dinner. When you do pick her up, she is a ball of excited joy who can light up the room with her smile. But the last few visits were cut off and shortened by more important things on your plate. When you bring her home three days early, she is a totally different child. Her manic rage and her expression of hurt are too much for a child to have to bear when it comes to emotional hurt. It is pain beyond my imagination for our daughter, and when she cried out and was just screaming,

"He doesn't love me, and he cares about other people and things and not me!" I could feel the pain in my soul that our daughter's heart was being broken by you, her father—not a strange little boy who broke up with her, but a man that has not shown compassion to his blood, his family, his angel, and his princess of a daughter. Sir, you are breaking your daughter's heart by not being present in her life and not loving her like your daughter, the love of your life.

So I am writing out of concern, care, and love on the behalf of our daughter, who loves you and needs you to be a father that shows love to all his children and family. Please do better with your daughter.

Thank you, and please hear her cry for love,
Your daughter's mother

Chapter Five

THE EVIL AND GOOD THAT MEN DO IS CRITICAL

As human beings, we all have the capacity to do good and evil things, whether we are conscious or unconscious of our behavior. Why is knowing this important? Knowing this is important because it makes the difference between the discovery of self and understanding the psychology of human behavior.

That is also why it is very important to know oneself! Once you understand yourself, you understand others too. The reality is that we are alike and that in many instances our differences are few. The difference between men and boys is choices. The choices that are made will follow us throughout our lives, and those choices will either help or hinder our ability to progress.

You see, making right choices is not an innate ability within all humans. The more education, experience, successes, and failures you have in life, the higher the likelihood of you making better decisions. This should give you relief in knowing that we all have the chance to do better after our mistakes occur. This is the truth! When we make decisions, there are always consequences that will follow, whether they be positive or negative. The choices we make should always be for the betterment of self and to make our families proud.

Each decision that is made depends on the intent of the individual's anticipated desired outcome. As men, we should always strive to make decisions that are honorable and that create better opportunities and promising futures for our families.

Men, it's important to know that we are relied upon, even when it is not spoken or well communicated. Why? Every family member is a contributor of direct and indirect talents of love, and it is not to be measured, but it is to be understood. One perception is that men within the family are held to higher standards as the protectors of the family.

Note that things will go wrong, and there are no perfect men, but it is imperative that we make the right choices and learn from the bad choices.

As men, we should know that when we make better decisions, it is to prevent us from going to jail or meeting an early death. The world is filled with tricks, false visions of reality, lies, and deception, and it is important that you strive to live a life without going to jail or meeting a violent death. If you have ever been in jail before or have made mistakes, you may feel as though no one trusts or believes in you. All you need to know is that every day you awake with breath in your body, you have an opportunity to make changes and right some wrongs.

Remember: your change is based not on your words but rather on what you prove and never repeat. Change is something that others see and believe based on what you do over a lifetime, no matter what the situation or scenario is.

You may ask yourself, "Who am I?" We are all good and evil, and what you do around others will allow them to see which side of you is represented. If you are a good person, then that is based on what you do and not what you talk about, and you should be willing to prove who you are. Talk is talk, and you have to know yourself. The evil that men do is usually done when we have no faith in our abilities, no goals to stay focused on, and we think that our families don't see us as trustworthy, and therefore judge us because of the bad choices that we have made in the past.

So when a man has lost sight of himself, he usually heads on a search for something that he needs, only he may have no clue on how to obtain it or keep it. Although all knowledge is power, it is knowing how to use the power when you find it that is key. This power is based on knowledge, experience, and whether the intent of the power is to do good or evil with it. Men, it's important that you know the difference between good and evil intentions, and strive to live lives of progress by doing the right things and keeping it legal.

Men, it is also vital to seek progress and change, because your family will honor you knowing you will bring prosperity to the household name rather than another con or trick. Doing this is not easy or perfect, but it can be done with self-control and purpose. However, it starts with admitting your faults and striving to do better. Having this in mind does require a strong mind that is able to withstand constructive criticism. Why? Just because you change does not mean that others have forgotten your past behavior. Having them believe that you have changed in your heart and mind will take time and your willingness to prove it without being upset but with the understanding that it will take time. But this is a step in the right direction toward accountability and being responsible for your own actions and becoming a real man.

Men, it is your responsibility to strive to be men of integrity, honesty, kindheartedness, and lovingness toward the family at all costs. Now, this does not mean that everything will be agreed upon or that everyone will do as you ask, but what it does mean is that your intention should always be to love your family through it all. Having this matured mind is not a show of weakness, but it is a responsibility that does require mental strength to endure. How you handle yourself is how well you will handle your family and life's situations.

Your ability to adopt this positive attitude will be based upon your ability to love and forgive. Love and forgiveness are necessary because they prove that you want unity, that you want to be on good terms, and that you want to restore a family relationship without division. It is possible for a family to be dysfunctional but functioning, meaning that there will be some good and bad times, because we are all human. For instance, people make mistakes and will do and say things that are hurtful, but it doesn't have to be unforgiving, because there is such a thing called love, and it exists today.

Love is something that society mainly talks about referring to intimate relationships, but there is much more to love than intimacy. I want to elaborate and say that love is like happiness. It is something that you do from within because you want to do it. Love is something you give in the hope that it is returned to you. Love requires patience, time, and a willingness to endure until it happens from the other person or situation.

In order for any relationship to work, you first have to start with your commitment to doing your best in all things. Know that failures or disappointments will come, but you must be determined to rebuild and prepare yourself to try again, but better than before. Don't ever give up on yourself, your family, or your friends because of differences. I want to encourage you to love them through it and to wait and let love be reciprocated in time. Allow your patience and understanding to be processed as they reveal themselves as the commitment of love.

When you love, you must also love yourself enough to possess a desire to commit, be disciplined and live life with a purpose. Commitment is the state or quality of being dedicated to a cause. It takes discipline to be committed, and the spirit must take into account that mind and spirit cannot be separated from the body in an absolute sense. What this means is that in order to live, you must be led by your inner spirit and mind with a commitment and desire to live. Men, this also means that you need to be driven by a greater power within yourself. Your commitment to live life with a driven purpose of importance will be beneficial to your family. To do this, you need a mind that is aware and focused at all times—not perfect, but aware! Why? You are needed, and your family depends on you to be present, and they desire for you to make them proud.

Howard Thurman, the author of the book, *Disciplines of the Spirit*, states, "If life is to manifest itself in a particular form, it poses the conditions, the discipline, essential to that end. A particular form of life is committed in a way to survival, a way of keeping alive."

I believe that if your mind is focused on the most valuable people and things in your life, then you should strive with a sense of commitment and do well, and that is the key. Men, stay focused! As a man, it is imperative that *you* understand that one of your quests on this earth is to protect your family at all costs and to teach them to do the same for their families. At some point in society, men fell short of the reasonable understanding about manhood, or perhaps a lot of men simply did not know this information about the importance of their role and their value to their families. It is important for both males and females to work together and to protect families b.

Men, you don't need permission to do the right thing! Protecting your family should be an innate ability that you know from just living. Unfortunately, this is not a truth that many embrace, but just as with all things, we live and we learn. I really hope that you understand your importance to your families and the world. Men, your presence is needed daily, and respect is given according to your ability to stand and endure all of life's encounters.

Men, it is very important to know that challenges are the consequences of your actions and the correction of your character to do better. Respect is given because you endure and demonstrate respect and love. The respect and love that you show toward others is your voice to make decisions within the family and prove to all that you are serious about your lives and concern about others. The correction is to help put you back in good standing with those you have offended and misguided because of your hurtful places in your hearts and minds. But through it all, forgiveness is the redemption and restoration of your hearts and minds.

Hurtful things have always been spoken about men and our positions, but now is the time to stand with our ladies and families and reclaim what is rightfully ours—family! Don't believe the hype, men, that we can live our best lives by ourselves. Why? Because separating and leaving our families is not okay, and it is the wrong action to take as men. Remember, men, when you leave your family, you are going against the order of the family structure.

Men who have left their families probably could not handle being the man or did not know how to accept the role of being a man. This is the very reason why I am writing this book, to break the chains of separation within families. When we better ourselves, we become major contributors to our families. Then we can build our families up to become better units of *one*.

There are no perfect families or parents, but there is a family that is perfect for you. Men, bad experiences are *not designed to cause you to fail*; they are for you to learn and to teach others so they can look at their situations differently too. Such experiences bring about awakening moments to invite in change for the better and to maybe stop these situations from happening to others.

We are striving to be happy and prosperous, but we have to endure the challenges and learn from our mistakes. Life is full of changes, and you have to strive to make it through those changes as though your life depends on it. Your family is your life, and the way you cultivate, protect, and teach others in the family to do the same will determine your level of respect and longevity that you have in and on your life. Honoring your parents and your family leads to a longer life for your family filled with love and admiration.

Men, if you want happiness and love to work, you must put in the work until it manifests itself positively. Happiness is created from within yourself first, and you should commit to finding happiness within yourself for it to work. Commitment, like happiness, is not based on others; it is based on your capacity to endure until it manifests. In other words, you have the ability to create it. But you must believe in your own ability to endure and demonstrate it by being a man of your word. Commitment is a state of being that one focuses on until something is done.

Men, you can change the mood of all things with the right mind state and behavior. Your family depends on you for your love, happiness, care, joy, peace, patience, leadership, honesty, forgiveness, rational emotional intelligence, and your ability to commit to things that you say you are going to do. Sometimes the problem is that we want others to do it for us instead of being responsible for ourselves. We think that if it goes wrong, everybody will blame us and say things like, "You call yourself a man?" Men, failure and disappointment are not designed to make one feel bad but to encourage one to change because there is a better way to do things.

Men, it is imperative that you become men of awareness, understanding, patience, and endurance. Life is full of hard times, and when these times arrive, you are to endure with wisdom, demonstrate your greatness, and show how passionate you are about making things work for yourself and the bettering of your situation. Men, please search within yourself to discover your passions and desires. Cultivate those things in these times of distress so you can lead yourself and your family as one corporate unit. It is up to you to lead. Surround yourselves with other positive men for encouragement and upliftment. Have around you other men who are older, wiser, family oriented, and positive. This is very important to your development as men.

Sometimes we become self-incapacitated as a result of not having a purpose or an understanding of the role of a man. In other words, an idle mind can lead to real life incapacitation, which will leave a family alienated and without a male, father, brother, or man. Having other mentors also helps with testing ideas on how to deal with life situations to stay focused. You have to find or make other ways to create the lifestyle that you want.

You don't need permission to be men, all you need is a better understanding of the value of you being present as men. In addition, men need the following abilities to be successful: a plan, the ability to endure, focus of commitment, forgiveness, and a godly or inspired mind to proceed to build themselves, their families, and promising futures. My grandfather, eight years before his death, often reiterated to me the importance of being a man, but for a long time I never understood what he was talking about. Now that I am older, I am understanding his words of wisdom. If a man is not thinking, then he is emotional; and if he is not careful, this can lead him into being an emotional wreck, which might force him to think about what was done. In my opinion, men should have ambitions about life that are cultivated and incorporated within his cerebrum.

A man's ambitions should be

- to protect and raise his family,
- to be spiritual and have a sense of moral values,
- to demonstrate prideful behaviors and to learn from mistakes,
- to create generational economic wealth and live debt free,
- to create or cultivate businesses or good work ethics, and
- to make investments for the family and expand into the future.

Men, your families are looking for long-term stability, and it is not easy, but it can be accomplished.

There are no shortcuts in life, so do the work with love, because it is your family. Remember: the children in your family are always watching you, and they will learn to be better than you were. This means that you have to be around to teach them and show them how to do it better.

Note: If a man does not have plans, then he can be a dangerous man to everyone, especially his family.

Men, Be Selfish about Life's Ambitions

In my first book titled *The Real Enemy: The Inner Me*, I stated the following: "Generations upon generations have been taught that being selfish is wrong and a behavior that we should change. This is true and it is misunderstood at the same time. For example, being selfish about sharing with others to help them is a selfish act that could be perceived to be wrong. We should all be selfish when it comes to our personal wellbeing, lifestyle, and future. It is true that no one will take care of self, better than self. In most of our lives we have been taught to be givers and not takers and that we must earn the respect of others. This is a situational truth and it is very important to know when and when not to be self."

When it comes to your well-being and life, it is great to be selfish, because when it comes to yourself, no one will ever be able to accomplish anything for you. Others can help, but no one can accomplish your personal success. You must come first in matters of your best interest for your life.

How does this impact your life? If you don't plan your own life, then others will have a plan for you, and it may not have anything to do with your will or destiny. "Know thyself" is an old African proverb that suggests that you should know yourself as a principle in order to survive, do anything, or help others out. Being selfish when it comes to your life is a positive way to help yourself. We as people must begin to understand that we can't help others until we help ourselves. Helping ourselves to reach our goals is the first step to a positive selfish act. It requires that you be goal-oriented and passionate about living a life of happiness in order to be able to help someone else.

It is imperative to work on self and establish yourself as an individual. Why? Because it will allow the opportunity for positive and like-minded individuals to become attracted to you and to connect with you, especially when you are out and about accomplishing and doing something as a contributor. Positive thoughts and behaviors will attract positive, like-minded people who are looking for others with a common factor.

Being selfish about your goals, ambitions, and inspirations about your life is not something to be ambiguous about; it should be something that's of importance and accomplished for self. Being able to make decisions about your life is essential and imperative to self, and you should be careful about whom you allow into your personal circle.

Men, it is critical that you understand yourselves and the vital role that you have in society as contributors to life, family, and your mothers and women. A woman is the greatest creation of life because of her ability to have children, which is the ability to give life. Without this understanding of self and women, it is going to be very difficult for you to understand others in your lives.

The following sections are designed specifically for you to reflect, self-examine, and then ask yourself, "What type of man am I to myself and to my family?"

Men, Understand Your Norms

Know yourself, be aware of your behavior and listen to your family and true friends about how you respond, because it does matter. Even though it is just their opinions, you must determine whether it is true or not. To know and to understand your norms for self-examination, you need to reflect on several things: upbringing at home, friends, and social and educational experiences. Human norms are not innate but are learned conditions with many variations that include parents, activities that involve your friends, institutional learning, elders in the community, family, life experiences, and words of wisdom. Regardless of how you learn, it is important to know that you will have to be conditioned so that you are not limited in your knowledge, and this will build your character both consciously and unconsciously.

The more we learn about life's circumstances, the more we grow to understanding ourselves. We all have the ability to act any way we want to as a child, but sometimes the childish behavior carries over into our adult lives. This inappropriate behavior can cause problems in the form of an underdeveloped mind and a lack of maturity in one's thoughts, understanding, and behaviors.

How will you know when to change your norms? First, you know that you need to change, but you choose to be comfortable with being a child because you have gotten away with your way of thinking and your behavior for so long. After a while, you really start thinking that it is the norm, but *you know it is not.*

If others are saying that your way of doing things is not cool or that it's not right, at some point you have to let it go. I think you really need to think about your behavior and wake up! You need to do better, and you really need to change. Why do you think like a child when your family needs you to be a man? If these words or phrases have ever been spoken to you, then you need to change your norms even when you don't think you need to change.

All this means is that your family cares for you and they love you. They also want you to be a man with courage, wisdom, and prosperity, because they rely and depend on you; ultimately, they desperately desire the family to be in good relationship with each other.

When you move in faith to become a better man, you will grow and emerge into a man of honor, trust, and respect who is loved because you decided to be better and raise yourself up. Perhaps you wanted this all along but were never comfortable enough to take this step and somehow managed to strive to improve yourself. Well, today is your day to move forward.

Men, Be Aware of Comfortable Norms

Comfortable norms occur when people accept their lives as they are and refuse to add more intellect to improve themselves or their lifestyles.

Being comfortable is another way to say that you don't need anything else. Most of the time when a person feels this way, it means that he or she is afraid of releasing his or her inner fears and thinks that he or she is protecting himself or herself from other people seeing his or her pain. This is dangerous, because not wanting to improve your character and life can be a hidden subliminal mask that could be hindering you from being greater, which to some degree is an alternate ego.

An alternate ego or personality that is adopted to adapt is one thing, but an alternate ego that is adopted to not change is a form of regression. Now, having an alternate ego to adapt until something better becomes your true personality is not a bad thing, because all of us mimic someone we admire because of his or her character and abilities. For example: Superman and Clark Kent are one and the same, but this being is seen during the day as a reporter and during heroic events as Superman. For many years I mimicked Superman's ability to do things fast with friends, and in school I was Clark Kent, meaning I was smart but did not let others know I was smart. Doing this is both good and bad. It is good because you can adjust and move forward in life, and it is bad because you have hidden concerns that could hinder your progress in adapting new ways and a better lifestyle.

In other words, your life experiences have value. Improve yourself and inspire to endure. Valuing yourself as a full embodiment of both good and bad is critical for you to know yourself. Why? Because you will need self-control to give you the power over yourself to think, act, and apologize when you need to, and to forgive from your heart. This is so important because, men, life matters!

Your life matters, and you have a lot to offer yourself and others *as they ask for your assistance.* Why is this relevant to *you* as a human being? It is relevant because your inner pain is attached to your gift and your passion, and if you don't learn to have self-control over your emotions, you can't realize your value as a person and a man. If this is ignored, you could become disillusioned about your being and the need for your presence within your family life as a gifted man.

"How so?" you may ask. All people are gifted, and our gifts are designed to be shown, praised, and increased with an awakening of wisdom. But the way you feel about your gift will assist you with how well you handle your situations of hurt. Everyone has hurt, and all of us have to cope with our challenged hurts, but knowing that you have an innate ability that allows you to communicate and make decisions will assist you with adaptation.

Men, I understand that being fixers is how we contribute, but fixing is based on you being asked to fix something, not on you volunteering your services. Remember: you can give only to those that ask for help and assistance. Why? When people ask for help, they are conscious in their minds and are more receptive of the help because they asked. Acting upon your impulse is normal, and most people think that they are helping with good intentions. This is an act that all people do, but be careful. Good intentions are not always accepted as good. Sometimes people who help without being asked to help come across as know-it-alls. It is better to listen and let people ask for help!

I believe that when this happens, you are accepting who you are as a gifted man. But don't be ashamed of being honest about things. Don't be afraid to be a good, honest man. Why? Your family needs you to be a contributor of love and wisdom. Men, do not become comfortable with your familiarity. People are not meant to stay the same; we are designed to evolve and mature into better human beings. This is true for all people. Being comfortable can also be a sign of being lazy, no matter who the comfortable person is. We are all to grow smarter, have responsibilities, and handle things in ways that do not separate our families, land us in jail, cause us to be homeless, or put us in the grave.

It is a great honor to be able to grow and mature as a man so that others can see you demonstrate you being *your* own man who loves himself and his family.

Men, Adapt to Change

Adapting to change requires being attentive and aware of yourself. What you have to offer others as a good, conscious leader is encouraging. My late grandfather Lawrence McKinley Jr. would always tell me to stop trying to change others and work on myself first, as the rest would be added to the value of my life. He told me to focus on becoming me and to surround myself with people who are doing good things to help themselves and others. Why is this important? No one will be able to save you, because you have to work toward saving yourself. Why? Accountability! Working in this way makes you accountable for your actions, plus it builds trust with others.

When you discover that honesty is the best practice, you will feel a sense of relief. It allows you to look inwardly at yourself, and it may require you to invest in yourself. You can try to enroll in a class or a course that focuses on time so that you can also improve your skills personally and professionally.

Personal development is an acute need for you and your life as a contributor to a society filled with a diversity of people in need of your wisdom and leadership abilities. You must change for the revelation of your life becoming better, which will align you with your destiny. There is more to us than we know, and ongoing education and experience will increase your awareness.

Knowledge gives us the keys to thinking, but what we do with it is entirely up to us. Striving to reach our destinies can be an ambiguous situation to figure out, but as long as we are committed to improving ourselves, with a focus on achieving, in time it will become clearer.

Destiny, in my opinion, is attached to your ability to become someone that you believe in without a doubt. What you sow you will also reap. If you sow well, it can be a benefit to your success and positive image. This state of mind should always be very important to your advancement in life. Becoming yourself and reaching your destiny has a cost, and that is change, which has to occur within your mind, body, and inner spirit.

The purging of releasing old bad and negative habits to advance and manifest a greater and respectable new way of thinking is priceless! There is so much riding on this taking place. You need to demonstrate that hard work pays off in the future. Men, never be afraid of adapting to positive change. Adaptation and change are part of the evolution of human beings. As you encounter the many journeys of life, at some point adapting to change will become a planned event every ten years, because you will come to the realization that it is hard but is necessary for your good.

Adaptation is a mental understanding about a greater intellect, and it will yield a decline in emotional hurt every time it is honored and supported by accountability. Life is a journey, and the mind is always in control of the body. As you matriculate in life, you transcend the growth of your mind and self-control of your thoughts, words, and actions in order to strive and meet your challenges at your best. In the end, trusted people will know and always look toward your continued advancement and your words of wisdom.

Men, be the best men that your families and the world will ever see. Be the best fathers, husbands, caregivers, leaders, and dependable men that you can be, and do it because it brings you joy, happiness, peace, and love. In return, you will create the opportunity for others to be influenced and encouraged to join in on the good and loving feeling that you create for them to immerse themselves in. Your triumphs and victories over challenges will make you stronger and wiser. Be the men that you've always dreamed of being, and never forget to adapt when it is necessary!

Men, Be Yourself

Being yourself should matter so emphatically that you should never stop striving to reach your full potential. The impetus behind you reaching your personal and professional goals should be a desire for betterment, which will change your life and give you direction and security. The higher you go, the higher your understanding and gain. Being yourself does not mean that you can be disrespectful or inconsiderate toward others, but it does mean that you should find a way to do things and remain in good standing.

Being in good standing can be another way of being truthful, but with consideration of how you communicate your thoughts. In other words, don't let ignorance overpower your thoughts of being humble to others. It is very important that you use your understanding and wisdom to grow rich in your thoughts and your leadership ability. It is stereotypical in the eyes of men and women that men should lead by example. Men should walk and draw others to admire their strength in their humility.

Although this can result in a lot of pressure, it should be seen as a good thing. Yet it is harder than the ideal because of the fact that over 44 percent of homes are fatherless and there is not a male to father the sons. I understand the childhood absences of fathers, but now that you are a man with responsibility, it is time to change, and that is why I have written this book. I did not have the privilege of growing up with my father, so I understand not having a father to give guidance, and I want to encourage you to trust this book as a positive tool to self-reflect and plan your life out for better experiences than what was given to you. Becoming yourself is essential to your life and is attached to you revealing your talents, skills, and gifts. Your gifts exist not to shame others, but to uplift others to do the same as you did for yourself and better.

Becoming yourself has another cost, as if you don't achieve in life, then it will be an expensive loss. The cost is your *life!* Your life needs to be filled with specific things, such as love, family, a career, and happiness. Without these necessities, you will be empty and your life will be filled with a void and a lot of second-guessing and what-ifs.

That is why being yourself is important to a purposeful life. To obtain these things will require some training, life experiences, and clairvoyance. And in time, when you least expect it, your passion will convert into your ideals and then gifts. These gifts are to be manifested so you can receive all that is designed for you. In essence, this is the cost of your life—your self-worth.

I will put it like this: Suppose an employer hires you to do a job and pays you according to your abilities that are on your résumé. Now imagine you open your own business doing the same thing as a self-employed contractor. Your worth goes up because there is no middle man, and now your value is triple what the employer pays you. Once you discover your value and worth, you are already walking into your destiny and becoming yourself to be yourself. So stop discounting yourself. This is a high cost that only you can realize and for which only you can create the opportunity.

As a man, it is time to believe in your abilities and to know that your gifts are also attached to your obedience, and you must do everything in your power to be successful.

What is the gift? Everyone has a gift, and the gift is the inner you that is connected to the Supreme Being, or the Creator, that will help you as you invest more to develop your gift.

A superior being or a creator is greater than all human beings, and even if you don't believe, just know that we, as humans, were created from a greater source than our parents, and even if we just keep living, life will teach us all that we need to know. Just do the research to understand that there is a greater being than humans and search for yourself so that you will know without influence, but of your own consciousness.

If you do believe that there is a superior being or a creator, that is great; and if you are not sure, then make sure that you believe in yourself and use your ability correctly for the right purpose and with a good attitude to make an impactful change.

Research different creation stories of humankind—for example, the Creation story in the Bible in the book of Genesis and Darwin's theory of evolution.

Being yourself is knowing your good and bad attributes, and your strengths and weaknesses. The rewards of discovering and knowing yourself are indescribable. Being yourself will determine how you build relationships. Being a good man is the only choice to make, and it is a journey that has its payoffs and its rewards.

We all have the ambition to be good. This is a desire that fuels us, and it is demonstrated through our actions that reflect efforts seen by others. However, there are many resources that are accessible that ensure gainful knowledge, such as reading books, attending or listening to lectures, watching videos of positive motivation, returning to school, and the use of the internet. Videos and face-to-face interaction are also intellectual activities.

These things and people are resources that can help keep us uplifted and motivated. Life is not a solved mystery! Life is to be discovered, and along the way there will be moments that will make you laugh, cry, be proud, be sad, and be filled with love and admiration. It is my belief that these moments are filled with activities, circumstances, knowledge and experiences that are intended to condition, expose, and improve your character. All experiences are character builders and life lessons. No one person has it all together; we are all broken and striving to be whole. But one thing that is certain to me is that we all have the need to be loved.

The secret to love is to give it from your heart without regrets, and without any expectations of anything in return. Some say that to receive love is to give it! Why? Because all of us will fall short on things and need a second, third, fourth, and fifth chance to do better; this is a fact that speaks to our imperfection. If it is true that we are imperfect as human beings, and you believe that has relevance to human nature, then it is to be considered that in order to receive forgiveness, you must be able to forgive. Forgiveness is an ability that is needed for effective communication.

We men suffer and cause pain to others and ourselves because of our mental and physical pain. Men, make sure that your life efforts of good and selfishness are not the cause of sorrow and death to your families and yourselves. Life is short, so don't cause issues for others with your poor judgment and inconsiderate mannerisms.

Men, for the next couple of weeks as you read and understand yourself better, try to find a way to cope with the myriad emotions that you feel (hurt, sadness, grief, depression, frustration, anger, and so on). Find some relief from the anguish that you feel you are in. You will find out that there are many coping mechanisms, but they will eventually fail because they are temporary solutions to deep problems. The real solution to any problem is the ability to self-reflect by analyzing truthfully. Although this is sometimes difficult, it's achievable through daily commitment and support.

Self-analysis is an arduous mental task that requires the personal actions of self-examination and self-control. Have a desire to atone and propagate daily with discipline in order to improve yourself. Remember that obstacles will come, and it is important to endure and reflect throughout the process. And do not forget to forgive, love, and grow personally!

Who am I?

In the book *The Real Enemy: The Inner Me*, I wrote on the importance of discovering yourself by presenting the question "Who am I?" The question was being asked, and is being asked now, because to my understanding, belief, and experience, once we discover who we are, then we can move forward with self-love, setting personal and career goals, and adhering to life's discipline with conviction to do well for ourselves and our families. As a man, it is important for you to know who you are, because your family, your community, and the world are waiting on you to present your unique contributions as a gift for us to marvel at as a human race.

"Who am I?" is a frequently asked question that has been asked throughout the world since the beginning of time. Discovering who we are is something that all of us must discover for ourselves. One evident way of knowing who someone is, is by observing how he or she responds to this question. Most of the time, it is seen through the behaviors that have manifested as a result of his or her choices. How is it that others can tell you who you are but you can't see your character or even your person? Primarily, we are doers and not watchers of ourselves, which is perfectly fine. But you should do things that you enjoy in life, which is the passion that drives us all to do well in life regardless of our personal situations and circumstances.

The question "Who am I?" is similar to "Where did I come from?" but is different in context and character. It is asking you, the person, what your role is in life and what you are going to do about it. Again, no one really knows the answer until we are dead, and then again only the living left behind will know that. One thing that is certain is that all human beings have character. The philosopher Heraclitus once stated, "A person's character is their fate." Our character is a reflection of who we really are as human beings, and as human beings we must continue to strive to both continually and daily become role models for ourselves and others.

We are contributors to life, we are doers and not hearers only, we are leaders who create paths for others, we are makers and inventors for new discoveries, we are one of many, we are the new that one day will be the old, we are the good that must overcome evil, and we are boys and girls who will one day be considered men and women. We are all human beings striving to become upright and law-abiding citizens to prove to ourselves and to the Creator that we can overcome anything we are challenged by. As human beings, we must face all of life's endeavors with the understanding that our challenges are our fears that must be conquered as each encounter occurs throughout life. One of the ways to conquer our fears and stay balanced with life is to set goals for ourselves and understand that the goals we set are the goals we achieve out of passion, joy, love, and peace.

Men, we were born to fight and dominate! It is time to wake up and fight for your lives and your families. You are the protectors, and it is important that you know this so you can ensure that the other males in your families fill this role too. This is part of the recycling of life, and it creates reassurance within the promise of a better tomorrow within the family structure. Remember this statement: if it is to be, it's up to me to make a difference in my life for a better me.

As a man, battling to exist in a misguided society that has perpetuated the idea that men are to dominate others is a false reality. We must dismantle this chain of thought, which has to be broken mentally and inwardly, and then we must be reeducated, and this will take time. Changing a mental perception is not easy, but it is necessary. All people are born to lead, to coexist, and to dominate the land to create a better lifestyle though relationships and strong communication. It is very important that we change our mindset, because we have captured this misguided point of view.

We are to strive to increase, achieve, and be better men and women. Communication is the strength of any relationship. Communication is the key to resolving problems on any level. It is very important to speak well. Why? Communicating to someone else about your thoughts, emotions, successes, and pain establishes a bond and a trust that ensures that you are both on the same page with clarity. Being on the same page is the objective with regard to getting people to relate to one another.

You are your achievements, with great responsibilities and success, and you are the mistakes you make along the way. As human beings, we must learn to accept the good with the bad things that we do, with the understanding that each of us must learn from his or her mistakes and never fall for the same mistake twice. We must expand on the successes so there is no room for being comfortable. You don't need to stop what you're doing to reach your goals; instead continually work to achieve them.

To achieve any goal in life, you must have the mental propensity, zeal, dogma, intelligence, perseverance, and willpower to provide measurable performance. This refers to the kind of results that manifest your speech to reach your audience over a period to impact them and employ change. Anything worth saying and doing is worth saying and doing well and with clarity!

CHAPTER SIX

YOUR LIFE HAS A COST! FIGHT!

To die a respectable and honorable death, you have to live a life full of purpose, respect, and honor.

The human fight for life is always for the future. At times, what is required for self-advancement is a selfish demeanor and the ability to change your way of thinking. Why? Negative thinking can be harmful and risky, not only to oneself but also to family and others in one's social circle. But being positive is healthier and is helpful for the human experience. Although we all do good and bad things, it is important to know that doing either has consequences. For instance, when bad things are done, there has to be correction, and through this experience we have to endure behavioral changes both mentally and physically in hopes to avoid the same mistake in the future.

On the other hand, being rehabilitated, reformed, and redirected for making bad or wrong choices is a direct act of love and concern about your well-being as a responsible person. Once you mentally mature and understand the importance of removing negative and deceptive patterns, things will begin to change. But goodness will not manifest without a daily fight. However, the changes to your behavior and thinking will require you, as a man, to put away childish and naive thinking.

How is this achieved? Well, it is achieved by you making better life choices for yourself, for your family, and for those around you. Just know that the mental fight will never cease, because it is an everyday thing, but it can be controlled with the right choices. You may ask why this is. Well, if our minds are set to stay positive, then we can do it, because we have an internal reminder to do better rather than to give in to bad behavior patterns. Then, and only then, can we better ourselves.

Men, it is also very important that we have self-control over our first impulsive responses. We must think before responding. One view about life is that you must be in control of yourself, which will, in turn, produce healthy relationships with others. That way you won't run the risk of destroying relationships with bad habits. The goal should be to have and maintain a better lifestyle, and to always invest in self-improvement opportunities. Why? It's important because we should all strive to have freedom in our minds.

Freedom is the power to act, speak, or think as you want without hindrance or restraint, and if you have freedom of the mind, then you will have the mental ability to let go of wrong thinking and behavior in order to produce positivity and goodness. With your pursuit of life in a better way, this act will be done out of love and truthfulness. With this in mind, remember that freedom of the mind is a lifestyle, not just a few habits.

Along with freedom is betterment. Betterment is the act or process of improving something. When you practice betterment, it is a sign that you take interest in self-care, which causes you to create an achievable life. This lifestyle includes a lifetime of self-improvement, and this should always be the goal. Remember that if your time and attention are focused on a better you, you don't have time for wastefulness. This means that you must stay focused on what is important.

Lesson: Trying to help or change someone else is a deterrent and a distraction from yourself, and the truth is that no one can change or help someone else until they help themselves. If this statement is true, then the reality of this statement is that you will never have that type of time, because it will take a lifetime to change yourself. I'm not being mean, and I am not saying that you can't give advice, but I am saying, you should take care of yourself! Why? Everyone has to walk his or her own path and encourage others along the way, but you should never let others' needs supersede yours. The only exception to this rule is for children under the age of eighteen who are under your care.

Be selfish about your lifestyle and achieving your goals first. I understand that we all fall on hard times, but the truth is that when we make a bad choices, we make them based on emotions out of concern for others. If your change has occurred, you can't put your expectations on another to change.

Your next goal should be never to dominate others, and this cannot be done without self-control. We must exhibit self-control over our negative thoughts and change our ruling behavior to that of encouragement. Trying to prove a point will get you nowhere, because positive and negative things will always coexist, but each person must choose the path that he or she wants to encounter. These choices are based off of knowledge, experience, and wisdom. No one is perfect or has mastery over life, but we all strive to be someone of importance and to shine when given the opportunity to manifest ourselves and our gifts.

It is important to understand the importance of being selfish when it comes to your well-being. As I state in my first book, *The Real Enemy: The Inner Me*, for generations upon generations we have been taught that being selfish is wrong and that it is a behavior that we should change. While this is true, at the same time it is also misunderstood. For example, being selfish about sharing with others to help them is a selfish act that could be perceived to be wrong. But we should all be selfish when it comes to our personal well-being, lifestyles, and future. It is true that no one will take care of oneself better than oneself. In most of our lives, we have been taught to give rather than to receive and that we must earn the respect of others. This is a situational truth, and it is very important to know when to be selfish and when not to be selfish.

Accomplishing personal success and having your best interest in life will almost always require putting yourself first for the sake of your well-being. While some will see being selfish as an arrogant gesture, it is needful to accomplish goals.

Men, it should be important to you that you begin to understand this narrative about yourselves. There is a need for you to be or become socially conscious people who are intentional about life, as well as to increase your awareness by engaging in real intellectual conversation and surrounding yourselves with others who share the point of view that you are striving to manifest. All men should strive to assets in the eyes of their families and should be heavily involved in life's decision-making process.

The society that we live in exists because of the people that live in the community, county, state, and world as contributors. Here are some basic thoughts on some inward hidden activities to be revealed:

1. **Sacrifice of meditation**: This involves speaking positively and speaking life over oneself through meditation or personal enrichment.
    a. Be able to motivate yourself to reach your goal successfully for self and family.
    b. Be able to serve and give, because serving is the act of doing for others, and the benefit is gratification and unforeseen positive deposits to self and others for a future need.
    c. Moving means leaving your comfort zones to move forward in faith to higher levels to create a better lifestyle.
    d. Stay committed, as your commitment is your word and your word is all you have in this world. However, it can be challenging for you to stay focused if you dwell in familiar places too long. These places can cause you to stagnate owing to the lack of movement of your mental and societal understanding with purpose, but remember that nothing remains the same and that you must have a purpose-driven life.
    e. Mentally staying alive and aware requires mental awareness. You also need to feel and believe that you desire a better lifestyle, and although doing new things is risky, know that there is a long-term payoff that will be gratifying and rewarding to your life and to those who serve as the beneficiaries.
2. **Seeking to show**: This means looking to strive emotionally and logically to take action steps in specific directions to find your new life and your new way of thinking. When this is achieved, you will discover a better understanding of your purpose and

will start to become fulfilled in your mind and heart through desiring happiness.

a. Seeking will take diligence that requires daily action. For this thought to become your reality, you must immerse your entire being until it becomes your reality. Because tomorrow is not guaranteed, it is just as important to stop taking your life and the lives of your family and loved ones for granted. Why? Because you are needed, but you have to put in the work. No one is going to do the work for you, because it is your life, and others will benefit from what you learn, create, and manifest.

3. **Talk is cheap and a con**: Talk is sometimes "proof" without evidence, and you can fool people who don't know any better. It is also trickery and conning. Without proof, it is all just a con artist's game full of deception and lies, and it does not make you worthy of respect.

4. **Gaining or acquiring:** What you give is what you will gain in life, and it does not matter the situation or the person. That is why it is so important to handle losses well and do things with the intent to inspire and assist by giving of your wisdom and your love.

a. In order to gain, you must have a plan of action, but you must discover *you*. Answer the following question for a personal in-depth inward look of yourself.

- Who do you want to be (in terms of a career and in your personal life as a contributor to self, family, and society)? Keep in mind that who you are today does not define your future self. Today is a condition, but tomorrow you can begin a plan to be someone else.

b. What are you willing to do to become who you want to be? Again, no one can give you your inner desires. It is up to you to work for it daily in order to achieve it.

c. Are you willing to change mentally to achieve what you want, and why is it important? Mentally changing should be done with a purpose through continuous education and exposure to improve your current lifestyle and relationships.

    d. Are you physically able to put in the work? Doing things differently and surrounding yourself with positive and like-minded people is based on the level of commitment that you have to have. To change requires self-control, patience, and the ability to endure and to accept life and people as they are. All of this should come without judgment and finger-pointing at others but rather with acceptance of other people as they are while you become the example that they need to see. Sometimes you, too, will have to endure criticism (feedback). These are changes that you will have to adapt to as you go through the questioning of yourself and your purpose while you are making worthy investments, such as your time and money, back into yourself.

    e. Do you have inspiration and spiritual time of reflection? Take time to meditate and to envision yourself in your new role. It is about your effort and your drive to implement each action daily even with all the challenges that you may encounter. You are worth the hard work that your investment will bring into your life.

5. **No shortcuts or instant gratification**: In life you have to have a plan of action, and it is important that you know that things don't happen just because you say them or think them. Nothing happens overnight. Daily you must plan, sacrifice, and have the drive to achieve. The intent to do and achieve will require the willpower to endure until it manifests. Your core purpose and intent as a man should be to take care of yourself and your family and, as a leading member, to ensure the future is bright for the children in your family.

6. **You have to fight for your life**: It is easy to fight when there are no challenges. The greatest fights occur when you have something to lose. The true fight in life is overcoming the negative and old behavioral patterns that you know are not what you need. We, as men, have to logically make exchanges in our thought processes for them to make sense emotionally to us, such as the following:

Old Habits	New Habits
Hanging out	Socializing (networking)
Not learning	Learning (school, business)
Having old friends	Having a new career and friends
Smoking and taking drugs	Abstaining from smoking and drug use
Excessive drinking	Drinking to be social; abstaining from drinking
Not caring	Caring for self, family, and others
Having negative thoughts	Having positive thoughts

CHAPTER SEVEN

MEN OF INTEGRITY

What you do when others are watching is great, but the true test of integrity is what you do when others are not watching. Eliminate the alternatives that motivate you and be what people see. According to the *Oxford English Dictionary,* "Integrity" means the "quality of being honest and having strong moral principle, moral uprightness." As a man and leader, it is important that you know that you are needed, and your integrity sets the standards for your family and sometimes for your friends.

Being honest requires communication. Typically, it is believed that men are not the most effective communicators. I know that we choose not to speak to avoid conflict and argument, and to keep from getting mad at others. I understand, and I want you to know that this is *your fault,* because choosing not to communicate to avoid conflict is the same as avoiding responsibilities. Let's deal with it. Why? Because others are dying and suffering because they cannot connect with you and don't know what to do, because you won't speak up and express your thoughts. Speaking also allows you to assume your place as the head of your family as a real man, though this does not mean being the head over others. Stop running and work on *you, your mind,* and *your ability* to weather the storms of conflict and the disappointments of life. As a man, your ability to provide is essential to your family.

It's a shame that men are letting women do the parenting and family communication to keep things together. Why are you sitting quietly numb, voiceless and disturbed? Women need our help, but they are vigilant and carry the weight of the family, children, work, and the world on their backs. However, they are doing a great job with style and grace. The main reason for this is that men are not doing it with them or for them. In addition, the woman loves her man, cleans, pays the bills, and still looks good, but she is also stressed. She is caring for everyone while the man is present but absent and enjoying the fruit of her spoils while being lazy.

If you are like this, then you must change and get your mind together. Men like this are known to have the mental capacity of a scared boy waiting on Mommy to kiss his wound and make it better. This is pathetic, annoying, and a disgrace to manhood, motherhood, and livelihood, because this is moving not forward but backward. Wake up and realize the value of your presence and your ability to withstand all that comes with being committed while showing integrity. Your integrity as a contributor to self, family, and society is much needed. You are one part of the solid foundation of the family as a strong stockholder and investor to demonstrate and lead in the areas of providing and protecting, as well as to show that you are a spiritual and God-fearing man, father, and human being. The need for your manhood is imperative to the family, because without you there is no balance in the family. Men, wake up and show your integrity and lead by example out of love and protection.

Dr. Henry Cloud, the author of *Integrity*, wrote, "While we would say that they all were people of good, 'character', the reality is that their 'personhood' all that was in their potential. Some aspects to who they were as people had never been seen as important to develop them in reaching the highest heights and all of the other investment they had made should have been afforded them." It is important that you build your character to empower your mind. This is what you were born to do on this earth. What is it that's holding you back from being a successful man and father? Stop using excuses as to the reasons why you don't strengthen yourself and serve your family's best interests in heart and mind. Every man has to come to the realization that he is great and to know that the world is waiting to see him come into his greatness.

The problem is not the expectation; the problem is that you don't want to do what's necessary because you think it is controlling. The reality is that the things your family is expecting of you are intended to help you be a better man so that they can be proud of your accomplishments.

No man is an island. If you believe you can do something and you put your mind to do, it will be your reality. As a man, there will always be situations that require you to accept what has occurred and to do things that others want you to do, and that's okay, as long as it is legal. What won't break you won't kill you. So do it and learn from it. Don't be afraid to venture into the expectations of others, as long as what you do is legal. The more you know, the better a person you will be. But your ability to do what you have to do to make a living will depend on your integrity. Your ability to reach higher heights depends on your ability to invest in yourself and to have the will to achieve your career and life goals.

The hardships that you encounter are not designed to break you. Hardships are designed to broaden your understanding about life and problem-solving from learned lessons. This aids in giving you a better understanding about self and life.

Men, watch your hurt places! Don't allow your hurt to blind the love that you want from your family, but fight for it and become a man that reaches the goals as a man and father. Why? Because it is in the best interest of the family. A man's integrity will take him a long way, and it will allow you to garner respect from the people in the world.

Dear Father,

I'm leaving this letter because we never talked, as you were so busy. I think I understand why you are busy all the time. So I want to take this time to say thank you for what you do for our family as a father, but there are some essential things that you are forgetting to do with your family: spending time, loving and showing love with engagement, having fun, and being able to go out and just be a family.

You have to make time for our family because we need you. Showing love to your family tells us that you love being around us. You help create our family. You need us, and we need you to show us that you want us to be a family. Having fun with our family is good for the family and comes from the heart.

Now, Father, I don't know if you know this, but women need a lot of attention. Mom needs your love as your wife, a lady, and your best friend.

I know I don't do certain things, but I'm older and I have friends. I watch their families have fun, break up, and divorce. I pray that does not happen to our family, because I would be stuck and I would resent you because of your choice to love work over the family that you made. You promised that we would always be a family. (No offense, but I would love to share my thoughts with you to prevent resentment.)

Father, you are the man, and you taught me that there is nothing that can't be overcome if people put their minds to doing it.

I love you forever!
Your son

CHAPTER EIGHT

THE WOMEN

W omen are to be protected and positively persuaded to be loved, not encouraged to engage in perverted behaviors, hated, or shamed.

The Name of a Woman

One of the most important things that every man needs to know and understand about a woman is that she makes sacrifices beyond our imagination for herself, her family, and especially her children.

Women are to be uplifted, not misused for sexual pleasure. They are also to be loved for their sexuality and essence. Men, our mothers, women, and daughters need you to protect them, not prostitute them. Men, this is one of our problems that has spiraled out of control, but we can do better if we want to. To change our minds is to believe that our women are a gift and that mothers hold the future within their DNA. Men, *stop* being the cause of the misleading of women, treating them like prostitutes and creating abusive situations that dismantle their character and kill their self-esteem. Men are to be providers for women and their families.

A woman has many epithets, including "queen," "princess," "wife," and "mother." The name that almost every woman wants is "wife." A wife is married to her husband forever in love until death parts them. The second name that rings like music to their ears is "mother." A mother is a woman in relation to her child or children by her husband or significant other. The man is responsible for being prepared to make this a reality called a family.

Furthermore, men, women are very beautiful, attractive, pretty, good looking, nice looking, lovable, inviting, magnetic, charming, pleasurable, pleasing, alluring, appealing, enchanting, captivating, fascinating to a man's eyes, and pleasant to be desired, but they are not to be misused, mistreated, and abused as if they are rugs to be stepped on by a man's ego and insecurities.

Men, treat all women the way you would treat your mother or a mother figure, and no matter what happens in the relationship, treat all women with respect and love. How you treat a woman is predicated not on how she treats you but on how you treat her in hopes that you reap good treatment in return. Why? The way a man treats a woman is not about the woman but about the male's behavior. A man's action and intent have to be proven to be honorable. Once you prove yourself, then lead by example and make sure you continue to live and endure until you get that same love in return. This is unconditional love.

A Woman Is More Than Her Appearance

A woman is more than her appearance. She has to be seen for both her physical beauty and mental (spiritual) understanding about life. A woman is the gift of peace and love, and when she is not treated with respect and consideration, she can be your worst enemy because she has been put in a position to defend herself. Hell has no fury like a woman scorned. A woman's voice of reason and rationalization is based on honesty, trust, emotion, and her perspective of how the situation appears to her. It is important to understand this message and learn to love women and treat women with respect. In return, they will love you and give your life more than you can imagine, with peace of mind, nights full of affection, and unconditional love.

Make sure you choose the right woman to love, because unfortunately there are some women that have thorns in their hearts, and loving such a woman will take more work, especially if you are not the guy that she respects and admires. There is a special mate for everyone; don't settle for less.

A woman is only as strong as she wants to be, but when things are not balanced and moving progressively forward as she would like them to be, she will become Ms. Independent, Superwoman, and she will use her super strength because she has no choice. A woman is also very transparent in her communication and in her abilities, especially when it comes to matters that need to be resolved in a certain time frame. The problem is that men do not always pay attention or listen to women when they are communicating and expressing the need for a situation to be resolved.

Women need for men to be attentive, conscious communicators and not problem-solvers all the time. This is hard for men to understand, because we are just not wired like that, but it is not fair for women to have to bear this by themselves. Why? Men don't always know the difference between when a woman is expressing her thoughts or feelings and when she needs us to do something. This in turn means we need to take action or problem-solve. Men, this is a problem we battle with internally and will probably continue to be challenged with, but the reality is that sometimes we just don't listen or ask enough questions.

Most of the time, a woman will tell you exactly what she is thinking and what she wants you to do, but there are times when the woman doesn't give her complete thoughts. This leaves us baffled about what to do or how to react. When you're not sure and are baffled about what to do, just say the following statements:

1. Do you want me to listen, or do you want me to do something?
2. I want to be on the same page with you, and I know I sometimes misread the situation, so please say that again.

Be attentive, looking at her eyes and listening. This does not emasculate you as a man; this empowers you to be a listener and trains you to understand women.

Being on the same page is a positive thing, but men, don't overdo it. Don't allow this type of questioning to become an excuse for a new bad habit; it will make you look like you don't know anything or have a backbone. Why? It will come across as if you are not listening and not being attentive. Why? She will know it according to her instinct, and it will try her trust in you as a sibling, husband, significant other, friend, or just a man in general. So don't play games, because this is not a game to play and you will be the one to lose out.

This also causes a breakdown of trust. Once this happens, there will be problems that were created by you and others through generations of dogmatic male chauvinist mannerisms that have degenerated the present woman as a being. Shame on men who comply with this type of thinking.

Men, when looking at a woman, on first sight, her exterior is noticeable, but what is missed is knowledge of the layers of her being and makeup beyond her exterior—her mind and her heart. In general, a woman is designed to provide life, support a family's needs, give guidance, manage the family affairs and household, love, nurture, and, lastly, protect what she loves, especially if she feels and believes it is hers.

A woman as a protector is no different than a man as a protector. To protect the family at all costs is a demand to ensure the family's well-being. Men, being in a protector role is a dual responsibility no matter the relationship status. Whether you are in a relationship with a child's mother or not, there is an innate calling on both of your lives. It is important to understand that a woman should never have to do things alone, especially for the family, or raise the children by herself. She did not make the children by herself. It takes two to have a baby. Men, if you are unsure of the child being yours, then get a blood test. A blood test can confirm that a child is yours, and this will eliminate any misunderstanding about who the baby's father is. It is better to have proof than to be uncertain about a child.

Men, when you think of a woman as the protector of the family, remember this: it is not that she wants this position; rather, these are the circumstances that she is left alone with or has assumed by default. A woman will do what she must do to take care of her family and children. In a relationship, the woman can keep things as a secret and a mystery because she owns her womanhood, and she may believe that not everything is to be told. This also increases her creative power to internally process things. A woman can change humanity through her ability to create human beings. This is a phenomenal thing that she can do, and it is beyond men's understanding. Women are also highly misunderstood, and the truth of the matter is that a woman is the closest to God's perfection on earth. I will elaborate on this later. A woman should be regarded as having high standards and should not be dismantled and dehumanized with words of mental abuse, mistreatment, treated as property, or physically abused. Men, we got this all wrong about women.

His Position—Relationships with a Woman

Men, when we choose a woman to have relations with or be in a relationship with, we should assume the position of a responsible man, because the woman should be able to trust a man at his word. Most of the time, a woman is willing to submit to a man as a friend, lover, and potential husband, but never for games. Most women want a man to protect her feelings, time, money, emotions, and body, and not take them for granted. When a man does this blindly, the woman does not know what is going on, but she gets a gut feeling. When a woman begins to feel and see the games being played, she will not stand for it. It is important that men *stop playing games with a woman's hearts.* No individual wants to be played, tricked, or have his or her heart tampered with or walked on by someone in the name of love.

Men, know that when a woman is in love, she is compelled to trust you because she wants to be loved, and she believes that you will do what you say you will do. A woman's concern is matters of love and well-being in the relationship. When you play with a woman's heart and the relationship does not work, it's *your* fault for misleading her.

Men, the love that a woman shares with you is out of submission to love, and that is all she wants from you. Men, wake up! One of the worst things that can happen to a woman is for a man to leave her—a breakup. When *you* break up or break her heart, it is important to understand the pain and suffering it causes her. She will do things impulsively and will sometimes act out of control. All this means is that men don't really understand women and have not been properly trained about how to have relationships or stay in relationships with women. Women are driven and have strong wills, determination, and power with or without the force of circumstances. When a woman has to be Wonder Woman, she will be, because it is required of her. Men, there are many things that can happen to you in plain sight because of a lack of attentiveness or listening to the situation, which can quickly go unresolved on your behalf.

What Men Don't Know Is Killing Their Relationships

It's important to learn to endure in all relationships. There are no perfect people in relationships. There are only people who want a good life, who strive to make a better living, and who want to be in love forever. It is very important, men, to know what you want so it doesn't come across as if you are playing games. That is why it is important to choose your lady or wife carefully, because she will move things around to be with you through the good and bad. But most of the time, a woman wants the same in return from you when she goes through her ups and downs.

It is also imperative that *you* stay in the relationship and learn to endure so that you can learn to communicate with each other. Yes, men and women mature at different stages of their lives, but that does not mean that women can't effectively communicate with you. Historically men have doubted and mistreated women for so long, as if they don't have minds of their own without men. Men who think like this are considered male chauvinists. That is why it is very important to be wise when choosing your friends.

Now, I do believe that if you choose that wrong person, it can be dangerous or can even end up in a terrifying and traumatic breakup, with both parties having broken hearts. Men, get to know a lady and bring her around others before having sex and marrying her, because being connected sexually and mentally with the wrong lady will never be bring about good results, especially if the woman is not on the same page with your goals, desires, and plans. This will cause more harm than love. If you are on different pages, competitiveness will come between you two, and one of you may have more expectations than the other, which will ultimately end the relationship because of differences.

If you're not equally yoked in lifestyles, goals, finances, and hobbies, it will bring about difficulty in all areas of the relationship. Therefore, it is very important to communicate when things will not work out, and the earlier the better. This will enable you move forward in life so that you both can find true love and happiness.

Friendship also matters more than sexual intercourse. Being friends means getting to know the other person. Get to know the woman and see if she is the one for you as a partner. I know this is old fashioned, but I have learned from my former relationships that I should have formed a friendship first; had I done so, maybe I could have avoided having to through a divorce. Why is this important? Sex is special sharing of two people's bodies that is attached emotionally and mentally within a marriage. The next phase is pleasure, and that encompasses embracing, attachment to the heart, and longing for one another. But the heart longs for love, not sex. So how can a man gain a better understanding about a woman and her needs from a man?

100 Ways Women Express Things to Men

Men, women have a negative perception of men, and it is very important to erase this stigma by improving your character. Here are a few things that men have been described as: angry, physically abusive, verbally abrasive, animalistic, prone to wanton violence, chauvinistic, manipulative, and selfish. If any of these are true about you, then it is time to change how you think, speak, behave. This starts with doing things with a purpose and being intentional about the things in life.

Men, I need to be transparent and admit that writing this chapter was very difficult for me as a man. Why? Because I am a man, and in order to speak about a woman's needs, it has to come from a woman's point of view. I was smart enough to realize that if I was to effectively give advice about women, it would have to have come from the perspective of a woman.

After realizing that I was not able to give a real point of view as a man, I wanted to ensure that this writing would be authentic to its essence. I took the liberty of collecting some data from one hundred random women of age twenty-one and older. The questions I asked were as follows:

1. What would you like men to know about being a woman?
2. What does a woman expect from a man?
3. What are the concerns that women have in relationships with men?

Below are their responses. Note that duplicate responses are not repeated.

- A woman is a born leader and produces leaders to lead a nation
- A woman is creative.
- A woman is designed to be a helpmate; that means the man needs to have something going for her to help and support with.
- A woman is strong, so don't misuse her or take her for granted.
- A woman can create and destroy.
- A woman loves a man that can cook.
- A woman loves a man whom she doesn't have to ask to do things and who does them just because.
- A woman loves a man who listens.
- A woman loves good sex and cuddling.
- A woman loves romantic gestures.
- A woman loves to be treated like a queen.
- A woman loves some spontaneous affection.
- A woman loves unplanned sex.
- A woman thinks from her heart and reacts with her emotions if things are right.
- A woman receives a man with his flaws; do the same in return and grow together.
- Women are powerful, so let us create life.

- A woman should not have to tell a man to take care of a home.
- A woman should not have to tell a man to pick up after himself, cut the grass, take out the trash, wash the car, or pump the gas.
- A woman sometimes does things to test you, but don't leave; just embrace her, as she is mad.
- Be a friend and do special things for a lady.
- Be clear in your communication and mean it.
- Be debt free and learn to manage your money.
- Be respectful and responsible to her needs, and it will favor you.
- Be serious when she is serious.
- Be smart in relationships and do not cheat.
- Commitment is important to a woman.
- Doing things with the children is not babysitting; it is your responsibility.
- Don't be a needy man.
- Don't call her another woman's name.
- Don't create doubt in a woman.
- Don't play games with a women's heart and mind.
- Don't start something that you cannot do all the time.
- Embrace the hard times and love her more, because she is weak.
- Get to know your woman.
- Give her girl time away from you so she can miss you and what you have.
- Have good credit.
- Have integrity.
- Have a long-term saving plan.
- Have makeup sex when the talking is over.
- Hug and touch her.
- It is the responsibility of both individuals to make a relationship work
- If she says no to your help, help her anyway because you love her, and tell that you want to help just because.
- If you don't know, say you don't know.
- Invest in her with a secure future.
- Know what women love.
- Laugh with her.

- Learn to love family first, not friends.
- Let women show you their love, and don't try to control love.
- Listen to her and don't solve a problem without her asking you to.
- Love is natural and is not controlled.
- Love is shown, not talked about.
- Love hard and love unconditionally.
- Massage her body regularly.
- Men, if you deposit into a women, know what you are doing, and if you're not a man leave a woman alone until you're ready to be a man
- Men just need to know what women want them to do.
- Men should be trained to endure and be prepared for marriage.
- Men should be more supportive and less threatening.
- Money doesn't show her love; it pays the bills.
- Never compare her to your exes or other women.
- Never lie; tell the truth out of love. She may forgive you.
- Own your faults, but only when they're yours. She knows when she is wrong.
- Engage in personal development.
- Put the woman first.
- Give yourself a reality check, and know a woman's expectations.
- Show her that she is yours in public.
- Treat her like a lady in all things, especially during hard times.
- Treat women with respect and they will respect you back.
- Trust is earned, and pleasure is the reward.
- A woman is attached to a man, and he should be proud of it.
- Women are complex and complicated when you're outside looking in.
- Women are more forgiving than you assume.
- Women are sexual beings just like men; they can slip up sometimes too.
- Women are worthy to have the best and are aggressive about getting it.
- Women need spiritual lifestyles, and men need them too.
- Women's minds are filled with imaginations.

- When she is upset, give her space.
- Your lady is not your mother but more.

Men, after listening, interacting, and reading over the above responses of the comments, I came to the conclusion that as a man, I have been lied to and I need to change some of my own ways. Men, we have been lied to, miseducated, and misled about women, creative ability, and the use of that power.

Men, it is very important to stop calling woman derogatory names that diminish who they really are.

Men, we need to understand that we have been historically lied to about women, and moving forward we have to change. We and our ways have caused women to endure mental anxiety and fall victim to stereotypes labels, which causes mental, physical, and spiritual enslavement only to please the male ego. This is not correct, and I want to say it and say it loud. Women have also been fooled to believe that they are beneath men, that they are property, and that they are sex objects that exist only to avail a man's pleasure and his desire, along with other unethical and immoral pleasures that lower the perception of a woman.

In my opinion, one of the worst things to ever do to any person is to limit a person's self-esteem and confidence and make him or her feel less than human. This stagnates the person's growth and delays his or her greatness from being manifested. Men, women have been burdened by the notion that they are good only for having children and providing sexual pleasures, but this is a lie. Although the need for them to be mothers and wives is essential, it is not the only thing that makes them women. Men, wake up! We have been lied to, bamboozled, hoodwinked, and fooled about the real value and greatness that women contribute to society. They continue to provide to our world the increase of businesspeople, inventors, doctors, lawyers, professional athletes, construction workers, and teachers. They also help populate the world and nurture children until they become productive citizens. Women matter to the entire world, and without women there is not a future.

The truth I have learned about women is that they are goddesses on earth under God's rule to inspire the world through their creative vision and work ethic. A woman should be held in high regard and given high status because of her gifts from heaven that allow her to love, manage life situations, and replenish the population. Men should embrace women more in all aspects of life. Both men and women should be ashamed of how they have created a negative image of how a woman is seen and treated. This shows there is little evidence that women lack confidence in themselves.

It is true that all humans have both good and evil within themselves, but when evil, bad or negative behavior is used, it is from being defensive. When a woman causes pain, wrath, and anguish, she feels as if she has to defend herself from dangerous opposition and feels that a person or people are attacking her. Who would not feel and be defensive! When a woman is forced into the act of self-defense, she automatically becomes a protector, and her mission is to act out of self-preservation and to remove the problem. She makes an executive decision. She does what has to be done, and the issue of right or wrong is not part of the equation at the time. A woman is human like everyone else, and no one is born to be a slave to any other person. This treatment of madness toward women has caused more than enough abuse and arbitrary behavior. The abduction of the female mind and disabling of her abilities to be greater has got to stop. No more kidnapping the minds of our women and their abilities to succeed and making them feel irrelevant, unvalued, or acknowledged as true competitors in the human war to be better people.

Here are some of the annoyances that have been raised against woman: she is the most disrespected person, she is the most unprotected person, she is the most neglected person, she is the most underrated person, she is the most abused and used person, and, lastly, she is the most underpaid, underprivileged, and underappreciated person. Men, we have to do better in how we view and treat women, because it is my belief that no one desires to be treated like a slave. *No one* is to be *enslaved*, and everyone desires to be uplifted and empowered to be good, better, and great.

Men, this abuse and abusive behavior have got to stop, and this starts with reading this book and passing its message on to other boys and men. It's important that men uplift other boys and men in order to reclaim, recalibrate, and reeducate the minds of men regarding women in the family and the relationships with women. No more derogatory name-calling. Why? Our mothers were victims of this abduction and raping of their identity through submission and degradation, and now it is time that we vindicate women in honor of all mothers past and uphold our current women and the future girls who will become ladies so they won't be victimized by the pervasive madness of men and women.

We can't change everyone at once, but we can start by spreading the word daily and with taking personal responsibility for our own actions first within ourselves, our families, and our awareness within our communities. Men, we have the power to empower our society to influence positive imaging, but it first starts with you. I do encourage you to change within yourself and then stand for what is right, which is not to enslave the minds of women by way of limitation and railroading them from being successful.

Why? When you know better you do better, and then you do things differently and better. Plus it's just the right thing to do now that you know. These acts of mistreating women have caused the hearts of women to turn to stone and have hindered them from wanting to be in relationships with men; thus, they turn to each other for comforting and affection.

These acts of mistreatment, in my opinion, are among the leading causes that many of our women think that they don't need a man. As human beings, we know that is not a true statement, and this has to stop. We all have been victims of hurt, discrimination, and prejudicial behavior, and although to some it may seem necessary, that is not true when you look at it from a moral perspective.

Our women desire better, and change starts now. Men, we are designed to be the protectors of women and families. We should encourage and enable our women to raise up to rule their lives by accomplishing goals. Together both men and women can strive to make a difference in the world against any oppressor or anyone who tries to disable the human race to be at war against the freedom and liberty of any person. No one is to be enslaved by another human being. It takes two to make everything happen and work, and it is important to apply this to everything in life.

Men, a woman is designed to be a loving, virtuous leader, a businesswoman, a wife, a mother of many children, and the family representative. It would be advantageous of us to inspire and uplift women as we would our mothers and ourselves.

A woman can elevate a man to greater heights in his achievement, and men must do the same for women because it is better to have two great people than one. A woman has the desire to do good things for herself and for the family. In this materialistic world, a positive mind and spiritual guidance, both mental and physical, will always prevail and be connected with family and those desiring her time and investment. A woman is a light to the world! She's not perfect, but she can be perfect for those people and situations that matter to her as valuable.

Men, human needs can be met if both a man and a woman work on building a legacy to secure the future for a family. I know this to be true because I look at the woman that are single parents, raising children, paying bills, opening businesses, and volunteering to help others with their needs. I know that if a woman can do it alone, she can also do it with the support of her man and family. This is life, and it can always be raised to be more abundant so one can live life to its fullest. All relationships should be producing lives of peace and harmony. Men, it is to my intelligent, emotional, and spiritual understanding that women are closer to God than men. Why? Because of the woman's innate ability to procreate. In my opinion, God and women are creative overseers of things, and nurturers of people and animals. They raise children and hope for the best of all humanity.

A woman is capable of moving mountains together with her family, children, or man, or by herself. Men, although we carry some of these innate character traits within us, we can do a better job in demonstration, and I want to enlighten you that women and men are capable of doing greater things with encouragement and motivation. Knowing this should be inspirational for all men. It is time to work toward erasing the lies that have driven us to separate from being families. Every person is given an equal opportunity to show and prove his or her potential to work and do well in life for the greater good of the family and self.

We are to encourage and empower, knowing that we can do more to inspire our families and help women reach their highest potentials. Why? We all reap the sowing of each other when it is done out of love and sharing with family for prosperity. We owe it to each other to do well because we are one human race and we should love each other and not be at war. So, remember, men: we are one human race. Love a women as you want to be loved, and treat her the way you want to be treated. Don't depend on her to tell you how to be a man; show her what a man is by always being present.

A Mother's Tree

A mother's tree is the beginning of essence for all things visible and unforeseen. A mother's tree is designed to give life to all who live life with purpose and breath. A mother's tree is the offspring of new buds that will soon blossom into a beautiful image of the mother. A mother's tree is one that is simple, with complexity, chaos, and love, love being the first intention and the last result of things. A mother's tree is the root of delightfulness and godliness in its purest form. A mother's tree is the abundance of life without vanity, strife, and vexation. A mother's tree is pure unconditional loved for all who desire to be loved.

CHAPTER NINE

MEN—PROBLEM SOLVERS AND HANDLERS

B eware, men, as these words will kill you or inspire you: "Maybe I'm not good enough!" This is the middle ground to the apex of your life.

Once you find your purpose, you are positioned to complete your task, which will change your life forever.

Man the Problem Solver

Life is hard and is filled with good times and problems. It is believed that all of us should face all things with the ideal of learning and mastery of self-control to have lifestyles of commitment and pleasure. This is a very important focus of introspection about self. Introspection is a vital necessity that all people should be seeking to increase personal development. The life journey you're on is for you to grow, mature, and develop yourself in all areas of your being: mental, physical, spiritual, and financial.

These four areas of development are needed to develop you to live. If you don't grow in these areas, then expect disappointment, and it will destroy your potential to enjoy family life and live an enjoyable lifestyle. It is important to always continue to develop your character to be a better man. If you don't develop yourself, then you prevent yourself from being in a better position to be successful, and that will be *your fault*. Blame only yourself for the problems you encounter that go unresolved. You were born to solve problems, especially when it comes to these next three areas, which are essential for life. Men, it is very important to know that your contribution and input in the family is relevant and needed.. Your role and position is to be a solver of problems and to be levelheaded. Now let's elaborate on the three problem areas that we must learn to endure.

1. **Family Problems**

   Family problems are always present, and as a man, the family relies on you to participate and to suggest and offer real solutions. The ability to communicate and be present is needed and welcome, but you, the man, must step up and engage to cultivate with the intent to resolve. Your intentions will determine your outcome. A man's ability to think situations through is important to determine how reliable he is to his family. When your family asks for your input, this is a good thing, because they love you and trust your opinion, and you have to be confident in your ability to give your thoughts. Even if your thinking is wrong, practice to improve your ability, and make it better the next time.

   Don't be afraid to be the man, because being a family man is part of your innate ability. Boys grow up to be men, and men become fathers either biologically or through extended family. Just being born into a family automatically gives you the opportunity to be a leader within your family. This is what you are born to do; don't let friends and society tell you any different. Don't get fooled by the choice and the evils that society offers, and don't let the absence of parents mislead you to believe otherwise either. These absences and misleading messages are due to many of the world's miseducating messages in history and the lack of wisdom in certain ethnic groups. That means that we have been filled with lies to control humans, which has led to us being used, being disposed of by others, and being afraid to be truthful.

Men, there is money being made off of the poor, and it is never spent correctly, but you need to know where it is so you can access it and use it correctly for the betterment of your family. It is very important that you understand the family dynamics and the importance of building and creating wealth to secure the future generation. Please take bits and pieces from the socialist and the capitalist points of view and develop the means to divide and conquer so you can build within your family structure.

Remember: within the family structure, you must be a leader and follow to have ownership and to achieve the building of an empire or kingdom structure. Here are some ideas, and you can also create your own: (1) a business or investment that generates funds; (2) investment in property or housing, farming with ponds, cattle, vegetables, herbs, or other foods; (3) investment in safety defense training or hunting equipment; (4) family unity gathering and discussing of plans (5) research of ways to make sure you profit from your investments and create residual income, disposable income, and charitable income; (6) having children and grandchildren and teaching them and developing them to do the same thing; and (7) encouraging your children and grandchildren to add other skills from their educations to add to the family talent and skill, and to achieve a return on investment to create family wealth. These are essential to living on earth as a human, but most people are only consumers and spend all their money, and that is okay, because it is an opportunity for you to gain from their spending with the products that others need. However, if you are wanting to build wealth, this is a starting point, so do the research and build. Be the man for your family and the future.

As a family man, it is imperative that you are aware of how you and the mother are to both be on board about the security of the family. That means that you should be the first on the scene at all costs. Your family is first. This is what you have been born to do have been prepared to do all of your life, and the problem is you.

You must understand how the cycle of life operates and functions as it pertains to each family member and his or her contributions to the family. It was for you to discuss with the family about business concepts and how to grow the family in business. You don't need to attend school, but you do have to be educated about business and find the people to help you achieve your family goal. Most men are not aware of this; otherwise, they would have better lifestyles and their families would benefit. Just because it has not been taught does not mean anything, but you will have to strive and be the first to break this curse of poverty. All the pieces must function as one calibrated unit.

Being a man who is effective at building an empire and dividing and conquering takes being focused on the well-being of the family for wealth and protecting each member that invests. If a man has a plan, he can handle anything that comes his way, but if there is no plan, there will be family problems as usual. With money or not, as a man, you need to know that you can handle anything if your intent is to love your family. Loving your family must be the intent behind all things that you do and achieve. A man's mind should be attached to his intentions and be demonstrated in his actions and felt in his communication by others; if the result ends with love and hugs, then the intent is honorable, with understanding and comforting. Men, allow your intention to shine, because that is what others will see and know about you.

2. Relationship Problems

The way in which a man handles relationships defines his character. All relationships have good and bad challenges in them, but how you respond to situations determines the amount of trust and confidence the other person perceives. Building confidence in others is about who we are. You have to breathe every day, but you have to be present to be known. The proof of who you are is in your behavior.

Being able to demonstrate who you are in a relationship is iconic in comparison to a potential friend, lover, spouse, or father figure; you must have fortitude and confidence. Be confident and comfortable in your skin, allow your personality to shine and manifest your truthful good nature, and work daily on being the trustful person that you are or that you desire to become. Why? Women already believe that the first time they meet you, they know who you are. They want to meet the real you on that occasion—not just a representative, but the real man. This means you must let the real man show up and always strive to change to improve yourself and not trick others into believing that you are something that you are not.

Although we all have good and evil character traits, you do not have to give in to the evil traits, but you will need to have self-control over your impulsive emotions and quick responses. Life is not based off of perceived notions of false gestures and words; rather, it shows that you are genuinely confident, vulnerable to your ability to be seen, and present as a man to overcome all things with the help of your family.

Being a man in a relationship requires being logical, thoughtful, insightful, resilient, and emotional. It's not about making things complicated or ruling over others with convoluted intentions or cultivating a fearful environment. Being able to handle relationship problems is about making things, including life, easier. You should strive to be the go-to guy and be the one that others in the family rely on. This type of understanding about being a man may require a change in behavior and is important to a man's character. The character of the man in a relationship is one of establishing peace and love through honesty and understanding, of being the voice of reason, and of being dependable and showing loyalty to the family's needs. The man must be able to cultivate the relationship and resolve the problems. Being the man does not mean dictating, but it does mean being present.

3. **Parental Problems**

Parenting can be a battle of the sexes because the egos of the parents get in the way, which causes communication problems. Whether you are living with the child's mother or not, it is critical that you learn as a parent to master the art of communication as it pertains to family situations and the well-being of the child. Communicating with the mother about the child's well-being, activities, and moral beliefs will be one of the most enormous areas of effectiveness that you will face as a man and a father. Why? The mother thinks that she is right, and she believes that she knows what the needs of the child are, and to some degree she is correct, especially when it comes to nurturing the child, but when it comes to logic and being task-oriented, responsibilities, and ensuring that certain things are done, that is your role. And you should know that the mother will check to make sure it is done. She checks everything because she is developing trust in you and the child. Why? At some point the mother wants to relinquish this responsibility to you and the child; then she can focus on other important matters. This should eliminate this myth about mothers and dispel its intentions. For a woman, to trust is easy, but when it comes to her child, her instincts are not always understandable—nothing against the father or anyone else in the family.

The child comes from the mother, and it is hard for her to trust anyone with her child, because of her spiritual, emotional, and physical connection with the child. The mother has a bond beyond the understanding of the man. So remember this: the man has to prove himself as a man and father in the relationship, and that means you have to prove that *you* are trustworthy and consistent in your interaction. This is intended to be disrespectful to any man, but know that the mother carried the child and experienced pain during birth, with the resiliency to live by the grace over her life to be a mother.

Men, you have to stay around and prove that you are in it for the long haul and that you will not run away just because times get hard or you and your partner have a difference during a conversation. Men, the stereotypical understanding about us is that we will have babies, will cheat, can't keep jobs, and will leave. So if you are not this type of man, then you have to do the opposite and prove yourself trustworthy, be consistent with your interactions in the relationship, and endure all things in the relationship until death do you part. You must be around and demonstrate your involvement and commitment to the mother and the family. Men, you have to give the woman time to develop trust, and time is not measured on your time frame but on her level of comfort. With the building of trust, she will become willing to relinquish some of the responsibility. Men, you just need to be available.

When a man leaves his family, he leaves a mother to parent alone. It forces her to have a superwoman complex or an "I don't need a man" complex. It is within a woman's desires to be in a relationship and in love with a man who wants to be in a relationship, but remember that a woman says things based on her experience and feedback from her girlfriends and parents to create a safety mechanism. She operates in this awareness in case the man decides to abandon the family and leave them for another woman, for a man, or to be single. Men, when we do this, leave the family—the mother with the children—to be vulnerable prey with no man at home to protect them from outside predators.

The family being vulnerable prey means that there is no man to protect, to be a watchman, or to secure and oversee the home, leaving the home open and available for any other person with the wrong intention to walk in and destroy a family emotionally, spiritually, and financially. Such people are known as predators. When we do this, there is no help with teaching responsibility to the children or helping with what families need from *us* as *men*. Men, wake up!

Be the protector, and don't get mad when the family and the child's mother are doing everything; just jump in, help, and jump right back out. Let the ego go, because this is your family, not strangers. Show the mothers of the family that you are wanting to engage, and do it from the heart. You don't need permission to engage. Know this: just because people in your family and your children's mother don't ask for help does not mean that they don't need help. If you see the need and you want to help, just jump in and do it, especially when they ask for your help. Always be in a ready position.

Remember this: women are very independent, and if you are not willing to prove yourself worthy as the man, then maybe you're not the man. But don't leave; just stay and work through your ego problem and learn as you go and talk to your mother or aunts about you ego. Be proactive at home as a loving man, and use common sense and do it out of love. I will say it again; a man does not need permission to be considerate. This can solve a lot of problems in your nonverbal communication and your engagement. Your family and the children's mother need to know that you are going to be around, and the way you demonstrate your love and care to your family does matter. Men, you matter! Remember: you must show love and speak love, but more so, you must be around to receive love from both your family and your child's mother.

Men, one of the top causes of divorce is financial problems. Your emotional support is very indicative that you have your finances together before you get into a serious relationship and definitely when you think about marriage or having a family with children. Money pays the bills! Money is a necessity in any relationship.

A man should always work toward how he can increase savings for future plans. Emotional support requires one to be there during the good and challenging times. Men, if a woman tells you that it is not all about the money because you can't buy her love, believe her. What this means is that she can work and take care of herself *right now*, but as the relationship grows and love develops, you will need to start getting your financial status together. Nothing is free in life, and you can't buy a woman's love, but you should not want to think like that. Just as a woman is independent and thinks like this, so should you be able to take care of yourself.

Women cannot be bought and are not to be treated like slaves or property, but they are looking for men that can provide for their families along with their income. This is a normal thought for a woman when she is in a serious relationship, but when she is not, she is very independent and waiting on the right man who can provide. Men, it is very important that you know this, because for some reason men think that all women are after their money, but that is not true of all women. Women that are after men for their money are like that either because they have been used by a man or because someone taught them this behavior to protect them and to get them to expect less from men.

Money is good in allowing you to be a provider and to ensure that you do your part in contributing in the relationship, and a woman should not have to tell you to do that. That means that you should be demonstrating this behavior. There are things that a woman needs, such as emotional support, a committed relationship, marriage, love, a man with a career that he can advance in, and financial security. This is the expectation women have for men, or what they refer to as "real men." When a woman starts talking like this, this is what she feels she is supposed to be thinking. The problem is that men are not taught, trained, or prepared to think about life and the purpose of life or to have families and prosperity. But this is what you are born to do—to be a man who wants to be in love, get married, and create a family.

Men, when you decide to be serious with a woman, these necessities need to be in place or you need to be working on putting them in place:

1. A vision for his life and a desire to support both self and family
2. Leadership and thoughts about future plans that include the woman and her plans
3. A strong work ethic to ensure financial security, and the will to protect
4. Family financial support and a desire to have children
5. A career, not just a job, as a career shows stability and security
6. A God-fearing, spiritual life or a belief system of moral and values
7. A social lifestyle
8. A car and savings for down payments for apartments or houses (or, if you stay home, savings for housing and a serious relationship)

Men must be able to

- act with integrity;
- be able to give and bear bad news;
- be creative;
- be fearless but enduring;
- be considerate of the feelings of others in their families;
- be teachers, coaches, and mentors;
- be truthful and honest;
- build a future for and with their families;
- endure in serious relationships and with family;
- do things with an intent for resolve;
- enhance their overall success;
- socialize;
- forgive
- give and take constructive criticism;
- give encouragement;
- handle emotions;
- have value systems;
- improve their power to give advice;
- improve their relationships;
- laugh, love, and show love;
- listen with curiosity;
- not judge but help;
- plan accordingly;
- be polite;
- possess financial management;
- put away differences and uncertain situations;
- rear children;
- show love and sympathy;
- show empathy, charity, and understanding;
- show endurance during challenging times;
- solve disagreements;
- solve problems and address complaints;
- speak with candor;
- take the time to cry;

- treat everyone in their families with respect and kindness;
- take care of the needs of others within their families;
- understand themselves and others; and
- use sound wisdom.

Men, you have to be aware of being distracted. Why? Because there are things that must be done, and you have to give your attention to them.

All men are problem solvers, so don't be the problem in your family or in society. You have to be strong in all aspects of temperament, because how you respond makes a relevant difference. Your presence as a man is needed, and without you there is no balance. As a man, you have to have the fortitude and attitude to endure all of life's unforeseen, unpredictable, and uncomfortable situations that may occur. This means being a mentally stable man.

Men are the balancers of their families, and women are the advisers and offer opinions on all things that are important. The woman, children, and family need you to be present with a voice of reason. The history of some men is that men are present but absent. This mentality has to dissipate, because in today's society, in which everything is accessible, it is important that men speak up and be heard only to bring balance, not to control or dictate.

Don't let the errors of the past or the present eliminate or emasculate you about anything. It is important that you become aware of your surroundings, your family, and society. This will help you to stay abreast of the importance of life so you can avoid disingenuous acts and manipulative emotions. Having this type of pattern in your thinking will lead you to think that you are not relevant to your family. This is not true on any level. Being a problem solver is part of your role as a man, and you have to show it and not just talk about it. If you want respect, then do things out of love and show respect daily so it is earned by those who are watching you and needing you to solve problems and suggest solutions. You are more powerful than you give yourself credit for.

You have to fight within yourself to be the best man, father, and spouse, because when you fight, you are proving yourself to be worthy, reliable, and dependable. As a man, it is important that you listen to yourself, your family, and your children, because they will have problems and will need you to be available to be the voice of reason in their times of need.

Men, stop with the self-affection, crying out loud for attention, and acting scared. This is a wake-up call! Why? Because you are needed. But if you feel as if you are worthless or depressed, please seek help from a counselor or spiritual inspirational person for assistance in your time of need, and don't be afraid to invest in your personal development. There is nothing wrong with personal development or counseling. However, there is something wrong if you continue to be the problem or if you don't think you need assistance when you know better.

Men, when you know something needs repair, you go to the shop to ask someone for help to get it fixed. So when you know, act like you know and do better. Men, please *stop* making excuses for what you can't do and demonstrate what you can do, and do it well as you learn to be better. No one is born to stay the same; we are born to evolve. This is what a problem solver is and what a problem solver is good for in the family.

Men, part of what every male that lives is called to do is serve and lead. Assuming the leadership role as a man and father is the highest point of understanding and knowledge. Men, wake up and solve the problems in yourself, your families, and especially your children. Solve the problems! Stop running away; love your families and embrace everything that happens and endure it unconditionally. You must learn to stay, stand, and endure, because if you don't, then someone else will attack your family. Beware! The power is in your hands. Men, wake up! Do the right things! Protect your families!

Men, you were born to lead yourselves, your families, and your communities. You must prove yourselves worthy and show that you will be consistent, never giving up on yourselves and your families.

To be a leader requires knowing how to lead with a purpose. No matter what your purpose is, you must be present and stay focused on your goals, and while remaining focused, you will eventually change.

Goleman, Boyatis, and McKee, the authors of *Primal Leadership*, quoted Keki Dadiseth regarding how he helped people to understand and act on new standards of accountability, and he took the time needed to follow some basic rules that can trigger changes:

1. Focus people's attention on the underlying issues and solutions to create common groups and understandings about what needs to change and why. By helping to articulate problems and surfacing the covert, hidden habits that people take for granted, the real state of the organization becomes a motivating force for change. Making the covert overt gives people a language to discuss what is working and what isn't in the organization and provides common ground to stand on while looking to the future.

2. Focus on the ideal, combining resonance-building leadership styles to get people talking about their hopes for the future and to tap into the dedication people feel for the organization. Connecting people's personal goals with a meaningful vision makes it safe to explore ways to reach the vision.

3. Move from talk to action. This starts with the leader. Bringing people together around a dream, moving from talk to action, and modeling new behavior is the leader's charge.

Understanding change and the need for all people to change with a purpose is critical. Change for the success of winning and protecting your family's well-being. Your success is a success that is shared with family as you are leading by example. You are never too late to lead and assume the responsibility to secure your family's future. For some men, I know this is the first-time hearing, reading or receiving this information about the importance of you, your change and what you mean to the family. For others, they may be in doubt of themselves because of hurt of lack of understanding about their role in life. Either one of the reasons this can and may have cause a deterrent and family separation. So, I want to reassure you that you are needed and that you were born to lead and all leaders endure change to reach their potential role.

As a man, your primary role is to lead your family with the woman as both of you attend to the children's lives and ensure them a future. Why? The secret that society doesn't necessary tell people is that your role as a man is to cultivate and build a family community with financial security. The determination to be respected and acknowledged is normal, and the top team or business executive position that you will achieve in life is arrived at through your family. You build your family through love, trust, patience, a plan, and financial investment.

Building your family requires being a doer and leading by example by doing things first. Talk is cheap. Remember this: when you as a human being, a person, a son, a brother, a nephew, a father, or a grandfather speak to your family members, some will respond in agreement or out of faith and belief in you. What am I saying? Faith is believing in an idea blindly hoping that it will manifest itself in the future. So make sure that you are serious about what you present to your family, because your family want to trust and believe in you and your leadership. Never doubt a woman, and know that a woman innately knows and understands the power of the family and the importance of having financial security. Men, wake up; you're needed!

According to Goleman, Boyatis, and McKee, the authors of *Primal Leadership*, "… emotional intelligence is intelligence regarding the emotions, especially in the ability to monitor one's own or other emotions." Men, you have the ability to make a great impact, but if you can monitor and control your impulsive responses toward other people, then you will be challenged by yourself to demonstrate it toward your family. This is a problem, and it is assumed that you have no self-control over your emotions and that you lack regard for others' feelings, emotions, and well-being. As a man, I know we don't deal with our hurt, but if you don't deal with your hurt, pain, or closet demons, you will continue to perpetuate this negative behavior against others, which means that you are causing this separation and self-destructive act. This type of behavior is inappropriate behavior and is never welcomed or accepted by anyone, especially your family. Family is all we have, and if we mistreat them, then it will be easier for predators to prey on them, because they will be vulnerable and seek attention and love from anyone or anything that looks or feels like love. Men, wake up! You are needed!

Men, it is critical that you let go of the emotional and mental entrapment that is holding you hostage mentally and emotionally. You should desire better than your hurt, and it is time to heal and live so you can recover. It is time to reflect healing and step into your leading roles as men and fathers for yourselves, your families, your children, and your communities as lawful citizens.

If you accept negative statements, thoughts, and stereotypes and allow them to consume your mind and behaviors, then you cannot break the chains of oppression and self-destruction until you change your perception of life.

On page 52 of *The Real Enemy: The Inner Me*, I define mental entrapment. Mental Entrapment is not an innate ability or something you are born with; it is a behavior learned through negative exposure. Mental entrapment occurs when you are not sure about self, life, or what you should be doing for yourself. It is sometimes created within the culture of your surroundings. Mental entrapment is a self-destructive act. In short, mental entrapment is the lack of the ability to tell the truth, admit the truth, and accept the truth about self, others, and situations.

The mind is full of optical illusions, and that is how we sometimes interpret life's situations. We tend to see things only in the present and to miss the failures of situations because we are taught to see only pain and to embed painful memories while our perception is deemed bleak and shady. This one conditional train of thought and this type of thinking is dangerous to the whole human race. Why? Because it creates a negative thinking process and behavior that can result in condemnation of oneself and others. It also can create a negativity that can slowly increase negative behavior and ultimately lead to sickness and decrease hope and the possibility of good things happening. This includes the possibility of good people entering your life that may be able to help you and assist you in your life.

This negative thinking process can appear in the form of revenge, depression, oppression, violence, avoidance, envy, and self-abuse. These types of negative thoughts create a negative character whose behaviors can also be dangerous to oneself and others. This thought process is self-destructive and will soon cause an elimination of self-image and self-esteem, and cause a distancing of family or friends. It could also lead to drug use and isolation from society, which could lead to homelessness, jail, or the grave. This is a critical process that is killing our youth, family, and friends.

Self-destruction is an act of indirect reflection about how you view yourself both inwardly and outwardly. Low self-esteem is the lack of confidence in self, and everyone needs a high self-esteem to compete in all areas and aspects of life, both personal and professional. Low self-esteem destroys the ability and desire to want to do well and could lead to serious mental and physical problems. Self-destruction is mental entrapment. Mental entrapment occurs when you can't let go of a past experience that has caused a negative outlook.

Always perceiving things with a negative perception can be toxic and is a hindrance to your personal and professional advancements within your family and career. Men, know this to be truth: the world is full of negative elements and people, but guess what? It is what it is, and there is no perfection in anything or anyone. You are the author and captain of yourself, and you have a choice to do well or let it go and suffer.

Choosing to do well means accepting that all things in life, both good and evil, are meant for us to deal with and learn from. Letting go means moving forward past a situation and forgiving but always knowing who you are as a person. Suffering is of the mind and body, which could lead to other dysfunctions and the breakdown of your body and very serious mental or physical disease.

Having a positive mind is very important for all human beings, but as a man you need a positive mind so you can be the rock and the builder of your true self. However, challenges are for us to work through, not to run from. You must deal with them so they won't hunt you mentally. It's time to release yourself from mental entrapment.

Our past conditions are situations, but they do not determine our future successes and outcomes. All things happened in the past to prepare us to help others in the future.

Although life is said to deal bad hands, it is imperative that we, as mutual minds, understand that we have the power of choice. Once you understand that life is based on the power of choice, then understanding, learning, and wisdom begin to create in you the desire to find yourself in order to become in tune with yourself, others, and your spirituality.

People are not meant to feel bondage; life is for people to realize and reach their potentials in order to fulfill their purposes and reach their destinies. Know this: what you think of yourself both inwardly and outwardly will be reflected in your behavior. We are all born to be great, but we must be willing and able to prove it by becoming good, better, and great. Life is nothing more than a competitive race for jobs, careers, and retirement, and the winner will be the best performer who trained and prepared to be the best.

There are some things that should be considered while training; they are personal choices. You must plan and save; you have to have the will to learn and be self-driven as an individual. This is one way of looking at self. Another way of looking at self is to remember that as children and adolescents we are taught in arithmetic class how to solve problems to get to the correct answers. In this same way, when problems, issues, and situations occur, we are not to deny, ignore, or run away from them, but we are to solve the problems. Problem-solving requires the *truth* about a situation. The truth will set you free mentally.

Men, it is important to plan your lives for as long as you are alive. Being present but absent is one of the perceptions that women have of men, and specifically of fathers that come around but are not consistent. Men, this is bad, because if you are present, then you should be present. Paying bills or child support does not mean that you are present. It simply means that you are taking care of one aspect of your responsibilities. The other part is being present emotionally. Participating and being available at important moments in life are also very important.

Men, you have to learn to endure and stand through the good and bad times, because your families need you to be present and show love within the dysfunction and through the family dynamics.

If you stand and endure, then you are a man; but if you leave and escape and turn your back on the people that you love and that love you, then you are a coward and you are afraid of dealing with life as a man. A man must be truthful about all things and must be able to deal with the truth in an understanding, questioning, communicative manner. He must have a desire to resolve, not to point fingers or to prove a point. He must do things out of love while learning from both the good and bad times. Why? Character growth occurs when you have learned from life experiences and education. Self-improvement is essential when it comes to building your character. When you improve yourself, you improve your character, which improves you as a man and father. Men, wake up!

CHAPTER TEN

MEN, FORGIVE

Forgiveness is the ability to release yourself from personal anguish in hopes of being peaceful with people that you care about, and specifically with the persons that offended you.

Men, it is imperative that *you* have forgiving hearts! Why? Because *men* need to learn to trust and to love themselves and others. One of the most difficult things for men to do is trust and love. Why? As a society, we have been conditioned and programed not to trust anyone, especially anyone who is not a family member. This statement holds true, because when you were a child, boys had to learn to protect themselves at school and in the community because parents were not always going to be around!

This was important to know because it was needed to raise awareness of the evils or bad people in the world. This type of training was intended to help boys and girls be aware and leery of strangers and lurking predators . This awareness was needed for males, especially fathers, because as they grew older, it was this type of conscious awareness that helped them to be protectors for their families.

Men, wake up! It is my opinion as a man that the quality of a man's character is determined by his ability to love purely; to exemplify courage, valor, honor, and truth in all situations; to make decisions without trying to be perfect; to show emotional support; to have integrity in public; to uplift the family name; and to be a financial provider to his family. In order to be able to do these things, men must learn to endure and celebrate failures and successes.

Men, learn to grow in knowledge as you encounter living as men and fathers. The payoff of knowledge and wisdom is not given to the swift or to the strong, but to those that endure over a period of time. Also, demonstrate that you want it enough to stay the course. Why? Because it is the prerequisite that is needed to be victorious over all things. There is a profound need for men to bring balance to relationships. I say this because there are myths that men with hurt feelings suffer from separation anxiety, which creates a lifelong stigma of low self-worth.

The Misnomer and Problem

As stated earlier, men are taught not to trust anyone, and this distrust is instilled in us as children. This has lingered over us from childhood and has transferred into our adulthood/manhood. And therefore, it will affect and infect our relationships as adults, specifically regarding romance and intimacy. Why? Because matters of the heart can confuse men when we have no trust to balance the emotional parts of our beings. We can become extremists, and for men, it can get out of hand. We will come from far left field with negative thoughts and disruptive behaviors, and we can become isolated. I know as a man that it hurts, and the feeling is lonely! I know that when a man gives his heart, time, and money to a relationship, it is new, emotional, and loving. The idea and feeling of being loved can also be terrifying, and we as men have to take our time to think and balance our logic against our emotions in order to make rational decisions and accept the love.

The inability of men to trust anyone has become a learned condition. The understanding of learned conditions is reflected in the theory of B. F. Skinner (1904–1990) that states that "the reaction (response) to an object or event (stimulus) by a person can be modified by 'learning', or conditioning." This conditional learned behavior is very impactful, and the truth of the matter is that whatever is taught during childhood may have a positive or negative affect.

Let's imagine the first time that your dating partner says to you that they want all of your heart and that you can trust it not to be broken. You become excited, confused and fearful and it is apparent. Then the partner says, I will protect your heart and that you can trust me, I will never hurt you and without a thought of doubt, you do it and it feels good.

At that time your feelings and trust level are high, and you share it with your male friends. But when you tell them, they begin to mock you and laugh at you. Then they say to you, "You are not supposed to be acting like a girl; don't you know you will get hurt? No one is to be trusted, and girls are perceived to be nothing but trouble, and when she is finished with you, she will move on to the next one." This can be both true and false. One man's experience is not always the same as another's, but there are some truths in this matter, because this can happen in any relationship that doesn't work out as planned. But that is life, and those are facts!

So don't try to control the narrative by saving your feelings; rather, have the experience and learn from your experiences with each person. Don't miss out on being in a relationship and experiencing love, because no matter what type of relationship you have, you are going to have challenges. That is a fact! Your whole heart belongs only to your spouse, and that is where I went wrong, because no one in my inner circle explained or lived a life that demonstrated this lifestyle.

The problem is not the distrust of others; the problem is not trusting yourself enough to endure the pain of life's lesson. But the point is to learn how to recover from all forms of losses in life, and to be able to recover from life's experiences requires a lifelong journey that everyone has to take in order to be okay with moving on. We must all learn how to deal with problems and learn how to move on.

Another problem is not experiencing life but knowing how to handle or adapt to real situations or circumstances that *will* occur in relationships that must be addressed and dealt with through understanding. Everyone will have to engage, participate, endure problems, learn how to understand, and forgive along the way when applicable, which is all the time.

Never forget that life is strange. We, as people, have to be willing to live life, laugh at life, and love through life and to forgive every time, but always remember not to despise wisdom. Men will experience both good and bad people, but it is evitable, but we must persevere with an outlook to having self-control and dealing with situations with an understanding—or the willingness to learn when we don't understand. This should be personal, so you can have balance and preserve your mental capacity for controlled behavior. Forgiveness is a necessity and a remedy to healing the mind, body, and soul or spirit.

Forgiveness is part of the human experience as we learn to endure, redeem, and restore broken situations in life differences with family and friends, as well as problems with our work or careers. When dealing with problems, it is important to listen and separate the truth from the lie and have a discussion. The objective should be to reestablish and maintain good terms with others, especially with all family members. Either resolve or respectfully end toxic relationships! No matter what you think, as a man it is important to know that you *must* endure all things without fear of failure or running because you don't understand or you're in the wrong. No one person is perfect! Stop thinking like that, and learn from your mistakes. The importance of endurance and experience is equivalent to that of understanding or wanting love.

With love you have to be able to endure both good and bad situations that occur and learn from those experiences in order for the relationship to continue, and this same understanding applies to life in general. *Love* demands endurance and experience from everyone that wants peace, happiness, and prosperity. Endurance is essential in all relationships and it is important to know that all people will make mistakes, including *you*.

When you are hurt, it can break your trust and even lower your trust, because your feelings are attached to your love. This can leave a void or hollow emptiness in your chest, but remember to accept the situation that happened and to forgive. For a lot of people, it is very hard to forgive; but the forgiveness is not for others, but for *you* and your peace of mind. So forgive and restore yourself so that you can grow and manage yourself and the relationship.

Forgiveness is not an innate ability, but we must simply just learn to forgive. Also, stay in your relationship, work through things, and move forward without being bitter or feeling hate toward the person that you feel caused the division in the relationship. It is safe to be upset and disappointed in yourself and others that have offended you, but don't forget to forgive, restore your relationships, and let things go for your peace of mind and healing.

Never forget, because no one should be a fool. Not forgetting means using the truth and experience as wisdom *and not* reminding the other person of the previous offense. Please don't allow hate and bitterness to consume you and turn into resentment or revenge, but remember to have self-control and to use wisdom as a cautionary reminder to not be fooled. Men, in all relationships you can use a bad incident as leverage and a reminder to encourage positive behavior or thought toward an individual or groups so it won't occur again. Control the situation or the narrative because you care about the other person and the relationship.

The most empowering thought is that men are needed and that to have the ability to trust and forgive is powerful. There is a need to give men hope to aspire to balance and harmony within their families and in relationships.

Forgiveness is the ability to release yourself from personal anguish in hopes of being respected and peaceful. The one thing that will block the ability to forgive is the lack of knowledge of peace that forgiveness brings. Men, please know that your ability to forgive is like your ability to lead, and if you abdicate, then you have some more personal development to do. Please understand that this is not an attack on your character but is an inspiration to add to your character for the betterment of yourself. Don't be afraid to change, because some things are very cut and dried, but it can be complicated. However, the resolution is to resolve situations for *your* peace of mind.

Moving forward, don't ever forget to understand that life is like a lake full of knowledge for one to obtain as one wills. The more you learn from life, the more knowledge you will gain. Remember that knowledge is a powerful and essential tool to gain. When you know what you know, then nothing gives you greater power and confidence in self than your ability to make decisions based on what you know. Having confidence in knowing the result of knowing is having confidence in order to continue to move forward without doubts.

Danger: As men, we must be able to submit and let go of some things, because doing otherwise could be harmful to ourselves or our families. Just be careful, because arrogance can show up. You have to watch arrogance because it can make you self-consumed in your mind with trying to prove a point instead of sharing or forgiving.

Jumping to conclusions without facts is an interruption that changes the direction and story in order to stroke another person's ego. So hear people out, and if what you are hearing is not favorable, then don't let it go unspoken. Always speak the truth about all things. Speaking about or discussing issues and concerns says that you are aware and care, especially if you are discussing issues with family members. Here is a communication example: "I think differently, and time will tell what the best decision that should be made is." This makes your position neutral, without agreeing or disagreeing. Men, when you are asked your opinion, present it out of honesty, respect, and love, and be intentional with your words while consistently speaking out of love and with peace. Don't deny correction when it's a serious situation, because your approach makes a world of difference while remembering to love and restore.

A Lesson about Forgiveness

All should forgive, because one day each of us will have to be forgiven, and forgiveness does not mean that one is weak. Furthermore, forgiveness gives you the ability to demonstrate and discuss things as a family and to bring situations to a resolution with forgiveness being the main point of emphasis. Forgiveness is the ability to release yourself from an offense or disagreement that could cause a separation from someone that you really want to be unified with. Forgiveness is not an opportunity to lie or be flaky about a situation, but it occurs after the two of you or a group have discussed the challenges and you want to be back in good standing with each other. Forgiveness is not about being right or wrong and trying to prove it. Forgiveness is totally about expressing your opinion and agreeing to disagree about a particular subject so that you can be on good terms despite the differences.

Men, build your families up in the understanding about family values, and explain the reasons why family situations, both good and bad challenges, will always be discussed out of love. Why? So each person can learn through communication and unconditional love. A forgiving man will use hugs and affection to demonstrate empathy and sympathy to comfort and support during challenging times. Fathers, you must also speak and demonstrate your affectionate love during the good times and be firm when problems arise through communication with the family.

Remember that there is nothing that you can't overcome as a family unit. It is something that you *must* do for peace within the family. Men, you can overcome any obstacle that will arise because of your mind and your ability to love, communicate, and build relationships. Family communication and love are needed and are important to create a tight niche that forms a family bond. Know always that issues may occur, but men, you have the ability to pull the family back together again with your words of unity, love, and knowing that family will have to endure moments like this. It is these moments that create the bond that is not easily broken. So remember that the ability to forgive is vitally important!

Men, there are also two words that you must strive to master through demonstration both mentally and physically. Mental demonstration means you must have a thought process and use knowledge to do what's good for family unity. Physical demonstration means you must be present and show actions that support family unity from a communication standpoint. The two words are "vanity" and "benevolent." I will explain how I use these two words and will define them for the purpose of clarity. Why is this important to know as a man? It allows you to relieve yourself from disappointments and heartaches from family and friends. How so? I'm glad you asked! Let me explain in my own understanding of the use of these terms and the value of these two words:

1. Vanity is the propensity to do something with an expectation. Vanity is vain, and there is nothing wrong with being vain about important things that you have an expectation of and wanting something back in return. That is also called being honest. The value of this behavior is that you're letting people know your intentions upfront, and this should prevent any misunderstanding in conversations or questions about your

position. This is your time to shine as a man and to be a man of integrity. Vanity is a principle that is easily misunderstood by many if it is not applied correctly and explained to those who don't understand the concept. Vanity is usually understood as selfish or negative, and it is truth.

Another point of view about vanity is that being vain means being honest about one's expectations from a situation that has value. Vanity is a great practice that everyone should be able to use by being honest with others about what he or she wants. Vanity is the key to being honest with yourself and others. In my opinion, vanity is good for those that seek to be truthful with others about selfish desires and expectations.

Unfortunately, as children we are not taught to understand vanity from this point of view, which is a disservice to us all, especially, when we want people to be upfront, truthful, and honest with us, especially about matters of the heart. This use of vanity will be difficult for others to understand, especially if a person lacks understanding of the word, because most people who want to be honest don't want the backlash that comes along with it.

Backlash is the thing that prevents us from being honest about ourselves and our desire to please others. So where is honesty? A lot of people say they want you to be honest, but it is not the best practice all the time, because some people are not 100 percent honest with themselves or others. This is referred to as being a fake, being a liar, or being pretentious. The excuse is that being honest creates a defense of shame for the person in question, who doesn't like the rejection or payback. Most people are not ready for the scary truth, and although being honest is the right thing to do, those that want to know the truth may not be ready to hear the truth. But as a man, it is important that you speak the truth with love and accept the truth from others with love and listen to their points of view, because right or wrong, negative or positive, and smart or dumb, everyone has a truth, and the drive should be to gain a better understanding and to resolve things out of respect and love.

When it comes to knowledge and wisdom, there are no rights or wrongs! There is knowing and understanding! Being mature means understanding that all people have knowledge, and some have more than others when it comes to making decisions. The proper understanding of vanity is the purest understanding of knowledge and wisdom. To me, knowledge and wisdom are knowing and understanding that all things exist, both positive and negative. Wisdom is prevalent in individuals who are being taught or seeking to know knowledge to improve themselves (spiritually and physically) and to be of assistance when called upon to be the voice of reason. Men, in many cultures we are seen as the voice of reason, not the dictator. This is your opportunity as the voice of reason to be heard, to be understood, and to be the neutralizer with truthfulness, honesty, love, and good intentions. Men, wake up to your calling and endure unconditionally when it come to the matters of the family and the heart.

2. "Benevolent" means "disposed to giving to someone or to a cause without wanting anything in return, not even a thank-you." The statement "giving charitably from the heart" can be misleading through wrongful thinking. There are some instances where we say that we are giving from the heart with an expectation (vanity), and there is nothing wrong with having an expectation; the issue is that you must make sure that you let the other person know that you want something in return. This behavior is exhibited in relationships, and it is perceived by women. Some women believe that men have ulterior motives and that that is why they are not truthful or trustful up front. Men, as leaders it is important that you demonstrate integrity when it comes to your families and spouses. It is important to have tactical ways of doing things, but be mindful of the conning part of yourself.

    Remember: all things have limitations. Understand that honesty is the best way of doing things and that it is a credit to your personality.

Vanity is the propensity to do things out of love with an expectation, but benevolence is the propensity to do things out of love without an expectation. Just make sure that you are okay with doing whatever it is and that your communication is clear so that everyone involved is on the same page and understanding.

But giving and doing things benevolently from the heart means truly giving genuinely from the heart without an expectation or a thank-you. As men it is important that we learn to separate these two concepts, because benevolence can easily cross over into vanity. For example, your wife asks for $100 and says that she wants to give it back in two weeks. You give it to her, and you tell her not to worry about it, as you are one and what is yours is hers. So she agrees to your terms. Two months later, you come up short on a bill that needs to be paid, and you go to your wife and ask for $100, and she says, "Let me check," and before she can finish checking, you automatically jump to the conclusion that she is going to say no. So you remind her of the $100 you gave her two months ago. She says, "I thought you gave that to me from your heart." So she gives you the money back, but now she feels as if she can't trust you and she is questioning whether she should ask you for anything anymore. Men, use your wisdom wisely in your giving.

Why is all this so important? It is important because we must know how to mentally apply trustfulness, our intention, and forgiveness. Men, this is very important for you to understand—more so than it is for women. Why? Men are perceived as being the rock and the voice of reason for the family, and most men are the backbone of a relationship. Men, your lives matter in your families, and your families depend on you to do the right things in life; without your presence and voice of reason, everyone is put into a vulnerable position and is subject to be invaded. You cannot leave your family vulnerable without anyone around to be the eyes, the ears, and the protector. Without you, the family is open to hurt, chaotic behavior, bitterness, hurtfulness toward one another, attitude problems, predators, drug and alcohol abuse, and any other bodily abuses. Your ability to forgive should be visible.

Men, wake up and accept your calling to be men with insightfulness while being the leaders of your families and role models to your children. Being a man is a calling that comes with great responsibility.

Men, love is a consequence. As men, you must be result driven, and the highest level of result is love. Being able to love requires the mental capacity to demonstrate affection and compassion. Love also requires endurance through good and challenging times, because you are being considerate of others' feelings and thoughts. Do this while speaking in the spirit of truth, being honest and kindhearted, willing to show a level of commitment to loving your family and showing forgiveness.

It is my belief that the psychology of forgiveness is that you must do something to be in good standing with another or others if you want to continue the relationship with the individual or group of people. Men, if it is your objective to be in good standing, there are times when it is up to you to demonstrate forgiveness. Why? Sometimes others don't know how to forgive. Forgiveness is not predicated on others but on how you demonstrate it, because it reflects your desire for the relationship to work. Remember: there is no such thing as a time table of when it is shown to you; there is only one day that we live in, and tomorrow is not promised to us. Why? Everyone grows and matures at his or her own pace, and learning is a lifetime series of events that continues to add to our knowledge banks.

Men show patience and endure while others grow, just as others had to wait on them to grow and mature. Having this type of awareness and understanding about self will help you realize that all people must go through a similar process. We are more alike than different, and the psychological understanding is that as a man, your mental and physical behavior has a great influence on those that surround you. Your being the voice of reason is a prized position to be entrusted with. This is also the greatest leadership position or fatherly role that you will ever encounter. Only your expansion of mind and experience can develop and improve your vision to help you achieve your manhood. But your greatness is formed by being present and enduring in all things.

So when your family and children have expectations from you, whether you are a success or failure, just know that they are still relying on you to continue to weather the storms in life. Your life depends on your ability to stand as an example, and no one is expecting men to be perfect in any capacity, but others are expecting you to do and say the right things out of love and concern. And if you're not able to speak your truth out of love, then you have to question your ability to love. Here is my food for thought about love:

Love is telling the truth and giving your opinion to support another person's decision, but it is not for you to get upset if the other person chooses an alternative to your suggestion. They, too, have choices, and the truth of the situation is always revealed. Do not try to be in control over your family or other people. They are not to be enslaved. Be understanding, and learn to be patient. Show love and always forgive so that the same good will be returned unto you at some point before you die. Even if it passes down in the family, you will be remembered as a forgiving man.

Having the ability to forgive is essential for you as a man, so when the time comes for you to forgive, then you should forgive and set the standards. But don't be a fool; discuss the seriousness of the offense and forgive.

Men, forgiveness means forgiving as often as one asks for forgiveness!

CHAPTER ELEVEN

A FINANCIAL MAN

A financial provider is one who provides money to support needs out of necessity. It is important to know that your financial perspective should be a contribution to stabilize your family's necessities. Men, your finances are for the building and stabilization of the family's basic needs and for investment in their future to strengthen opportunities for ventures and creating wealth.

Wealth-building for your family is a process. Invest in learning to create a goal-orientated family. Discuss a family plan and create a goal chart, become organized (by writing out how everyone contributes), implement the investment plan (by creating a vision board and tracking investment progress), and, lastly, duplicate your efforts (by training your children to do the same thing). Men, the greatest investment you can make is an investment in your family, and the greatest thought about this plan is based on your leadership and plan, so take the lead and work with other family members to ensure the unity of the benefit.

Men, as financial providers and family men this should increase your confidence in knowing that your family trusts you and your plans. Now, if you have tried this but you lost your family's investments, then you need to just follow someone else's lead or make sure that your mind is right and your intentions are in the right place. Also, make sure that you have the best interest at heart for the family and any future children. This confidence-buster is one that a man can always rely on, because even women and children want their men to be pack leaders and the heroes of their families.

This is an innate response with an expectation from both parents until one of them relinquishes his or her power and decides to mentally, emotionally, and financially leave the family or give up the hopes and dreams of the family and himself or herself. If you do this, then you will have to communicate and be all the way in.

To prevent hopelessness, you must be all in for the right reasons as you contribute personal finances and add to the family's success. The correct state of mind is important, and it should be focused not on control but on doing things out of love. Why love? Love is equivalent to being loving and kindhearted.

As a man and financial provider, it is very important that you understand that most family problems and marriages end because of financial problems and the lack of effective communication. According to a recent study by the American Academy of Matrimonial Lawyers (AAML), "communication problems were the number one reason for divorce in the United States. The study stated that about 67.5 percent of all marriage failed, because of a breakdown of communication. The reasons for a lack of communication include arguing, the inability to understand the other spouse, or total lack of communication."

Men, it is very important to have a career and a healthy lifestyle. I was once told that a man can't eat if he does not have a job or own a business. Throughout history, men have always prided themselves on working and providing for their families. Every man should desire to have his own money so he can do what he needs to do. As a single man, having money is very important for dating, going out with friends, traveling, and saving money for the next stage of life, which can include preparing for a family.

A family man should also be focused on security in preparation for his retirement. As a financial provider and family man, it is very important that you know that your mother, aunt, sister, daughter, and wife all look forward to you contributing and being stable in your finances. It is a natural response for women to support or lead, and it is of no offence to men.

Why is it important for men to be positive and strive for even better?

For self! One thing that is for sure is that, as a man, you need to be selfish about the things that are valuable and the things that will allow progress to transform in a lifestyle that yields personal success.

Personal selfishness will allow you to do things for self-satisfaction, which is very important, as it pertains to being confident. This is a must for every man, because we must be willing to do things for self and for the benefit of our families. Why? When things go wrong, it is very important that a man be himself and be patient with the process until things turn around.

In order to help someone else, you must first help yourself. For men it is important to demonstrate this character during times of challenges that could dismantle the stability of the family. Men, it is also important to be settled through your affection as a loving man.

It is imperative that you know that not everyone's intentions are in your favor, and that includes some family members. Everything you do should be based on love and trust in the family and other relationships that you have established. Therefore, I want to invite you to make this a personal rule: depend only on your own abilities and listen to others' positive and constructive advice.

Positive, constructive advice is good. Why is this a valid point? Sometimes we give our greatness away, and then we become comfortable in accepting being second best. Don't get me wrong; training is good, and you should be always willing to be trained as an investment. Why? After the training, there should be advancement, and it should happen within the time frame of a few years. The reason for this is simple: you have to value your self-worth enough to want to advance yourself. Being good does not just require saying that you are good; it requires the ability to prove it to others. Good is not self-proclaiming; it exists only when others witness your achievements.

I would like to reiterate a point of view about being good that I stated in my book *The Real Enemy: The Inner Me*:

> To be good is the objective for everything in life. For example, you make a mistake and the lesson learned is to correct the mistake by doing it right, good, or better the next time. Good is a natural state of being!

It is bad that is unnatural! Bad is so unnatural that it can turn into a disease or it can be an opportunity to transform. It is your viewpoint. Mental Notes: An opportunist seeks the chance to strive and to create their life with greater possibilities.

It is so important that you accept roles of leadership and be a strong and disciplined follower at the same time. To achieve any goal in this life, you must first have and understand honesty, discipline, commitment and dedication. These are the foundational tools for success. So set your goals high and operate with faith. Believe in yourself until it is accomplished internally, and you can duplicate it externally.

Your financial contribution is very essential to the growth of yourself and the family. Your money is yours, but the money should be used to support the family. Why? Your parent or someone supported you from birth until you graduated from high school. If you had no parent or foster parent, someone was in your life. If you are self-made and you are aligned with this information, you should continue to follow the instruction use this information to assist yourself with establishing the value of understanding why your finances are important to your family.

If you and the mother are not together, whether you're working a job or not, it is your duty to play a role in your child's life both emotionally and financially. Emotional and financial support are equally important, and as a father you should feel obligated to offer both. Even though there are hardships, the least you can do is be there emotionally for your child your with time while you are you are looking for a job or career.

Men, understand that helping and being there for the child is not an option but an obligation and a relief to the mother. The child and mother are still family; just because you are not together does not exclude either one from the family. This is a mature understanding of being a man who cares for his family.

Child Support Case

One of the most difficult things for any person is not being the custodial parent (the parent that the child lives with daily) but having to be put on child support. I agree, but I do want to shine some light on the situation.

There are both fathers and mothers that are challenged by the fear of being forced to pay child support. So I want to elaborate on the importance of paying child support and not keeping tabs on what the custodial parent does with the money. Child support is paid to help unmarried or custodial parents meet the care needs of children.

In an effort to direct resources in cases where collections are possible, and to ensure that the custodial parent has more control over whether to receive child support services, the court should give a ruling of this kind of case by the state. The ruling should be evidence-based and should result in families receiving more consistent payments of child support. It is also intended to improve the accuracy and the compliance with child support orders. If not, then a state child support agency will increase case investigation efforts and develop a sufficient evidentiary basis for child support orders.

Through this process, cases can be reviewed, and the process can be made more transparent by making the review results available to the public, as well as by allowing parents opportunities to provide meaningful input, to seek reviews to adjust the child support orders, and to help to reduce uncollectible debt, participation in illegal income-generating activities, and recidivism.

When it comes to child support or child custody, most cases focus on the child's "best interests," which means that the custody and visitation decisions are made on the best situation for the child's happiness, security, mental health, and emotional development, as well while he or she transitions into adulthood. The court's main objective is the child's best interests as the child maintains a close and loving relationship with both parents, which can be difficult but is not impossible if both parents' objectives are in the best interests of the child as well.

Unfortunately, when there are differences and custody conflicts, it's crucial to not lose sight of the importance of making decisions in the best interests of your children. Why? The choices you make today will affect your children's development and lives. According to several state laws and organizations the "best interest of the child" standards are as follows (I compressed several of the best to make them easily understandable in simple terms):

Best Interests of the Child

- The fitness of the parents
- The character and reputation of the parents
- The natural parents' desires based on any agreements between them
- The possibility of maintaining natural family relations
- The child's or children's preference if old enough and able to make a rational judgment
- Material opportunities that will affect the child's future life
- The age, health, and sex of the child
- Where each parent lives and the feasibility of the noncustodial parent visiting
- The amount of time the child has been separated from the natural parent who is seeking custody
- The impact of a prior voluntary abandonment or surrender of custody
- Any special needs a child may have and how each parent takes care of those needs
- Religious and cultural considerations
- The need for continuation of a stable home environment

In cases of joint physical or legal custody, the court considers the following:

- The willingness of each parent to share custody (including whether or not parents can or will communicate)
- The psychological and physical health of each parent
- The bond between the child and each parent
- The effect shared physical custody will have on the child's social and school life

- The geographic proximity of the parents' homes
- The demands of each parent's employment
- The number of children involved and their ages
- The motive behind the parents' request
- The financial status of the parents
- The impact on state or federal assistance
- The benefit to the parents

I know that it can be difficult at times, but once a child is born and you claim that child as yours, then your role as a man, father, protector, and financial provider is activated. It is very important that you strive to get your life in order as a man and choose you reckless activities wisely. Also be aware that your behavior will be known and acknowledged by the child and spoken of within the family.

You have the power to control the perception of who you are as a human being, a person, and a father. No one can control your character, your behavior, or your words. It is important that you know this, because your child will always need you to be present despite the parental relationship. You have control over your fate, and if it is in the hands of someone else, then that is because you chose to be subpar and a slave.

Men, wake up and realize the importance of your being needed within your families, your communities, as society as a whole. However, keep in mind that both men and women together make the world go around. One without the other is a road to the extinction of humanity.

Men, be all your business, and never mind the struggle while doing so, because in the long run, the payoff is rewarding. No matter how hard life gets, don't forget that it is designed only to correct the wrong within you and to push out the good in you. This is so you can be seen and heard through your lifestyle rather than just through your words.

Men, in order to achieve greatness, you will have to travel a road with bumps and heartache. However, each lesson that leads to healing, happiness, and self-gratification comes into your lives so that your families will be proud of you. Family does matter!

LETTERS / NOTES

The following letters written are to help identify family situations that are serious and have real implications. The intent is to bring about a consciousness to inspire a cognitive process that provoke a positive change when it comes to parental and children relationships. The letters are inspired by actual truth.

Dear Daddy,

Thank you for being at my graduation. As I have always been told, now life begins. I first want to say that I love you and I know that you love me too. What I am about to say to you, you may agree or may not agree with. I have made my mind up in regard to a specific situation, and I know that he loves me and we are going to do this. I would tell Mom, but she will find out sooner or later, and she is going to need support really badly, because this will cause problems that she will not be able to handle or understand from our point of view.

So here it is. I am in love with an older man that has always treated me well, with respect and honesty. He has been waiting for me to turn of legal age so we can be together in a real relationship. Dad, he is so much like you but more, because he has shown me for years how much he loves me. Plus you're my dad, and he is a man with a different set of desires. Dad, when a woman becomes of age, she needs a man to consider her needs in almost every way possible. Dad, he is 6'3", he is a handsome American with an Asian background, and he works on computers in IT. He also has his own home and his own car. He loves to travel, and he loves me.

So, Dad, I'm writing this letter because after my graduation and upcoming trip to Vegas this week, I will be married. I will be moving out on my own, and I will not be returning home for a while. Mom does not know this, and I'm depending on you to share this letter with her so she will know. I know that this is a surprise and that this will break both of your hearts, but this is happening, and I just want you two to love me and my choices.

Okay! Now here comes the questionable news. Again, please love me for my choices. In thirty minutes, I will be married and he will be my husband. Mom won't understand our love and how deep it has grown for years. When Mom would get mad at him for no reason, I would comfort him. When she kicked him out the house, I would let him in my room through the window to sleep in my room.

We have been in love for as long as I have known him, and he has never let me down. When you did not take care of me and mom was short of cash, he would take care of my needs. He takes care of my every need, as a man should. I remember what you told me as a child; you said that one day I would find a man that would take care of me and love me for me, and that is what he does. I love him, and I love you, too, Daddy. Please don't be mad at me or him, because we are both to blame. If there is heartbreak, please try to be happy for my happiness. We love each other, and you and Mom are great parents. I love you both. Please share with Mom and tell her I'm sorry, but we are in love and I still love her.

I love you, Dad!

~

Dad,

I love you! I know that I should know better than my actions show, because my mother did a good job teaching me.

I have called you many times, and I have waited by the door, the window, and now in my room for you to spend time with me as your son—and your firstborn at that! I left countless messages, and the most recent was four days ago. I texted you to come and see me today at 4:00, and you said, "Yes! I will be there at 3:30 and on time this time." You promised, and I said to you that my life depended on it and that if you didn't show up, then I would tell you why my decision was made. You still said, "I promise I will be there, on time, and I love you."

Dad, if you're reading this letter, then you did not come and you broke your promise again, and I am out of your way. I hope you know that you don't have to make any more promises to me that you can't keep. So here is my message to you: I love you and I wanted to spend more time with you. I was begging you to spend time with me because you told me that only a man can raise a boy to be a man.

Now I am out of the way, and this is the message. Please don't neglect your other children, because you are the father, and your job is to protect us and teach us how to be independent. I understand that you've moved on and that you and my mom are not together anymore, but I was not supposed to be in the breakup. I am your flesh and blood, your son, and your firstborn child. You said that I was your everything. What changed?

This is your fault, because I've cried for four years for you to spend more time with me, so I hope you learn from this message and mistake, and I hope that you love all three of your other children equally so they can be better children in a relationship with you.

Please don't treat your other children like you did me; don't neglect them. You were my first hero, and I loved you, but a sacrifice had to be made in order for you to open your eyes. I hope that you change and realize in your heart that you erred as a father in many ways. Please do better. I'm out of your way now, and you are free from me. My heart does not have to hurt anymore, and I hope that I get to heaven, because I really did try. Bye!

Love,
Your son

~

Dear Father,

How are you today? I'm fine! I just want you to know that you are a terrific father and that I wish I could have had more time with you instead of being alone with my mother. My mother is a sick person who doesn't know how to treat a child, and I was blamed for everything wrong in her life and all of her problems.

I'm not perfect, and I can't do all of the things she wants me to do with others. Father, I'm tired, and I also feel that I can never meet my mother's standards for a respectful girl or lady. So I am confessing to you how my mother has been forcing me to be her personal assistant and to do things that I am not proud of as a girl. This has been ongoing since I was eight years old, after you left us.

Father, you stopped talking to me, hugging me, picking me up, planning things with me, and paying money to Mother. When you left, things changed, and my mother had to adjust to the changes. At first she was just mad and yelling at me about everything, and then she had parties, and strange people were at the house all the time. One day a man came into my room! I tried talking to Mom, but she did not listen.

She would change the subject and talk about how you left us and you didn't care about us anymore, and that we had to find a way until a better way came along. It got bad, and I lost my innocence as a girl at the age of ten. This went on until I was sixteen.

Father, I'm tired of living and doing this. I don't have friends, and I'm not going to school anymore. I am having ongoing affairs. I have had some losses, and Mom said that we didn't need another mouth to feed.

I am writing to express myself to you in your absence, and I am so sorry for not being good enough to be loved by you. I blame you for not caring and loving me as your daughter. You should have covered me and mom as a husband and a dad.

Love,
Your daughter

~

Dear Mother,

I love you for giving me your all, but you didn't hear my cry. I asked you if I could live with my dad, and you refused to let me. You reminded me that he doesn't deserve the opportunity to be loved by me and that he left us and didn't care about us. However, at that time you were being selfish, and I know that it was needed, because you did everything for me.

Mother, know this (with no disrespect to you): a woman can't teach a boy to be a man. Only a father can, and that is what I wanted and needed as a boy.

Please don't be mad at me, but the truth had to be told. Now I am on my own, and I will grow up and try to build a relationship with him. Mother, you did a great job, but you are not a man.

Thank you, and I love you.

~

Dear Dad,

I love you, but I don't know how to say that you weren't more than just words. You showed me no love when I needed it. When I asked for you to make time for me, you still didn't. I have run away because my mother's boyfriend has taken advantage of my innocence as a girl for the last five years and I have no one to save me but me. I thought that you loved me, and I thought that you were going to protect me like you said, but you didn't. Now I am scared for my life, but I will figure it out.

I love you, Dad.
PS: Why didn't you love and save me like a soldier or a father?

~

Dear Dad,

I first want to say thank you for teaching me as I was growing up; I'm sorry for not listening to you when I was younger. Now I'm sitting in jail, and I have been thinking about the first of many times that you told me not to touch things that aren't mine. You said that touching things that aren't mine is stealing and that people go to jail for doing that. I admit I should have listened to you, and I'm sorry for not following your instructions as my dad.

When I get out of here, I would like to come to you and let you help me get my life together. Jail is not for me, and I want to do better. I know that I will have to prove that I want to change. It will not be easy, but I believe it will be worth it.

Dad, with God and you on my side, I can do all things as long as I stay focused.

Again, I am sorry.

Love,
Your son

~

Dear Father,

I'm leaving this letter because you are always busy. I think I understand now. So I wanted to elaborate on my point of view regarding what I call the key essential things to know and not forget: time, love, family, and fun.

Time: Make time for your family, because your family needs you too.

Love: Showing love to your family is saying you love being around them.

Family: Your family need you to show that you want to be around them through all situations.

Fun: Having fun with your family is good for the family, your heart, and the children.

Father, I don't know if you know this, but women needs a lot of attention. Mom needs your love as a woman and a wife. I know that I don't know certain things, because I'm seventeen, but I have friends, and I watch their families have fun, break up, and divorce, and I pray that this does not happen to our family. Father, when you chose to love work over the family, I became upset, and I felt unliked or unloved. (No offense, but I love you enough to share the truth of my thoughts).

Today I am a husband and a father in those same shoes. I'm learning to do better than my childhood experiences.

The truth builds character.

I love you.

∼

Dear Father of my child,

I know we have our differences of opinion on things; that is certain. I also know that your daughter loves you; that is a fact. However, I am writing this letter to you because I know the kind of a man you are as a father and the love you have for your angelic daughter.

Your daughter is eleven years old and is very aware of things, and her mind never stops going. She is formulating her own opinion about you in your absence. She has also expressed that she does not feel loved by you and that she thinks you don't love her because you have a new family now.

Every day that you call or text her stating that you are coming to pick her up, she literally sits by the window, waiting to see you show up. When she realizes that you are not coming and gets tired of waiting, she goes to her bed and cries herself to sleep without eating dinner.

When you do pick her up and she's expecting to stay a week or a few days with you, something always comes up, and you bring her back home early. She cries in her sleep with an attitude and screams, "He doesn't love me and he doesn't care about me. He only cares about others and cares about that girl's children more than me."

You are slowly breaking your daughter's heart by not being present.

So I'm writing out of concern, care, and love in hopes that you will see past the pain of our past relationship and begin to spend more time with your daughter. If not, you will be the first man and male figure (her own father) who breaks her heart.

Love,
Your child's mother

~

Dear Mom,

I love your for taking care of me! I really do love you for that. Thanks! But Mom, you didn't listen to me when I said I wanted to go be with my dad. Instead you lectured me on staying focused on school and life at home! You'd say my future and career count on the things that I do today.

So, for the last five years, your friend took advantage of my innocence as a girl and dared me to say something. He told me that this is how a girl becomes a woman, and I believed him. .

You did not pay attention when I asked for you not to leave and asked whether I could go over to my dad's because I didn't like your boyfriend. You would yell that I needed to get used to him being around because he was the love of your life.

That is why I left. I will find my dad, and I hope he is expecting me. Love you, Mom.

~

Dear Father,

I can only say this the best way that I know how, so here it is. You and Momma were always arguing about money, and I was sad. Every time you two argued, I would leave and go over to a male family member's house. While over at his apartment, we would drink and smoke, and then I could relax and calm down to return home and go to bed. I'm telling you this because I'm not going to live with either of you anymore.

One day, as I was over at his house to get away, he kissed me and told me this was what he did with all family and that it should make me feel better. After a while, he played country music and movies about men, and he kissed me when I left. I didn't mind that kiss, but when he showed me two men on TV, I did not like it; nor did I understand. So I told him that this was weird, and he said that this is what strong men do to trust each other as family.

During my last visit, he showed me a picture of man in love and showed me how to love a man. He suggested afterward to always be in love with a woman, and I told him I didn't feel well, and I left. He asked me not to tell.

Now that I'm older, I realize that he took advantage of my innocence as a boy, and I don't trust him or other men anymore. If I see him again, I might harm him because I am angry. So I pray every day for a peace of mind. I just thought you should know, because my wife and boyfriend said that I should say something, and I needed to let it go.

PS: I'm messed up, but I will be okay!
I love you!

THE MOST DANGEROUS MAN

The most dangerous man is the man that believes the lies about himself and that he is and will never be anything or that he is no good.

The most dangerous man is the man who is a father and believes that he is not needed by his children and is a deadbeat.

The most dangerous man is the man that does not fall in love with being responsible.

The most dangerous man is the man that doesn't love himself enough to realize he is a prince and can be a king.

The most dangerous man is the man that does not contribute to himself, his family, and society.

The most dangerous man is the man who is alone and believes that his life does not matter.

The most dangerous man is a father that won't be responsible for self, family, a wife or girlfriend, children, or family.

The most dangerous man is the man that doesn't believe in self, love, and life.

The most dangerous man is one who can't see himself in his children's eyes, to love at any cost to be their dad.

The most dangerous men don't care and give up on themselves, family, and life but are still present.

The most dangerous men don't show wisdom or help their families.

Dangerous men don't speak.

Dangerous men need to wake up, because families need them to be alive.

Dangerous men are hurt men that need a family to comfort them.

Men are needed to love, respect, and support their families and to protect them from dangerous people in society.

Don't be the most dangerous man that believes he is not one of the most important beings on the face of this earth.

Without men and women together, there are no children and the future is extinction.

MEN, WAKE UP!

BIBLIOGRAPHY

Single Mother Statistic. March 12, 2022: https://singlemotherguide.com/single-mother-statistics

American Academy of Matrimonial Lawyers (AAML)

Blankenhorn, David. *Fatherless America: Confronting Our Most Urgent Social Problem*. New York: Basic, 1995.

Children-ourinvestment.org. "Teens and Toddlers: Children Without Fathers." *Teens and Toddlers: Children Without Fathers*. February 9, 2010. http://www.children-ourinvestment.org/T&TStats-ChildrenWithoutFathers.html&gt.

Christianity Today. "The Fatherless Child." *Christianity Today*, October 2007. Accessed: April 27, 2010. http://www.christianitytoday.com/ct/2007/october/29.25.html?start=1&gt.

Dad's World. *Parenting Statistics*. 2007. Accessed: February 9, 2010. http://www.dadsworld.com/parenting-statistics/importance-of-fathers.html&gt.

Fathermag. *Fatherless Homes Statistics*. *Fathermag*. February 9, 2010. http://www.fathermag.com/news/2756-suicide.shtml&gt.

Father's Day DC. *Father's Day Statistics*. 2002. Accessed: February 9, 2010. http://www.innocentdads.org/stats.htm&gt.

Northouse, P. G. (2001). Leadership: theory and practice. Thousand Oaks, California: Sage Publications.

Goleman, Daniel; Richard Boyatzis; and Annie McKee. *Primal Leadership: Realizing the Power of Emotional Intelligence.* Boston: Harvard Business Review Press, 2013.

Kriesberg, Louis. *Mothers in Poverty: A Study of Fatherless Families.* New Brunswick, New Jersey: Aldine Transaction, 2006.

McKinley, A. D. *The Real Enemy: The Inner Me.* Self-Published: Anthony D. McKinley, 2014.

Peck, M. Scott. *The Road Less Traveled.* New York: Touchstone, 2014.

Popenoe, David. *Families without Fathers.* Piscataway, New Jersey: Transaction, 2017

———. *Life without Father: Compelling New Evidence That Fatherhood and Marriage Are Indispensable for the Good of Children and Society.* New York: Martin Kessler, 1996.

Rhodes, Kristina, and John Pattison. "Rescuing a Fatherless Generation." *Relevant Magazine,* December 2, 2009. Accessed: April 27, 2010. http://www.relevantmagazine.com/life/relationship/features/19214-rescuing-a-fatherless-generation&gt.

Sabrina. "Statistics." *Fatherless Generation* (blog). https://thefatherlessgeneration.wordpress.com/statistics/.

Thurman, Howard. *Disciplines of the Spirit.* Richmond, Indiana: Friends United Press, 2003.

Merriam-Webster.com. 2011. https://www.merriam-webster.com (8 May 2011).

ABOUT THE AUTHOR

The author wants men to search within themselves to identify the underlying issues and deal with them and focus on the real-life value of life, which is family and being available if permissible. The author wants men to use the book as a self-help resource book that provides ideals, suggestions and give thought provoking information that will help with reflect and perception about the core meaning of life which is: God, Self and Family.

Printed in the United States
by Baker & Taylor Publisher Services